First World War
and Army of Occupation
War Diary
France, Belgium and Germany

2 DIVISION
6 Infantry Brigade
King's (Liverpool Regiment)
1st Battalion
1 February 1915 - 31 December 1915

WO95/1360/1

The Naval & Military Press Ltd
www.nmarchive.com
Published in association with The National Archives

Published by

The Naval & Military Press Ltd

Unit 10 Ridgewood Industrial Park,

Uckfield, East Sussex,

TN22 5QE England

Tel: +44 (0) 1825 749494

www.naval-military-press.com

www.nmarchive.com

This diary has been reprinted in facsimile from the original. Any imperfections are inevitably reproduced and the quality may fall short of modern type and cartographic standards.

© **Crown Copyright**
Images reproduced by permission of The National Archives, London, England, 2015.

Contents

Document type	Place/Title	Date From	Date To
Heading	WO95/1360/3		
Heading	2nd Division War Diaries 5th Battn Liverpool Regt. Joined 24-2-15, From 1st February To 31st December 1915		
Heading	2nd Division 6th Inf. Bde. War Diary 5th Battalion Liverpool Regiment February 1915		
War Diary	Canterbury	01/02/1915	21/02/1915
War Diary	Havre	21/02/1915	23/02/1915
War Diary	Bethune	24/02/1915	25/02/1915
War Diary	Vendin-Lez-Bethune	25/02/1915	28/02/1915
Heading	2nd Division 6th Inf. Bde War Diary 5th Battalion Liverpool Regiment March 1915		
War Diary	Vendin-Lez-Bethune	01/03/1915	02/03/1915
War Diary	Pont Tournant	02/03/1915	08/03/1915
War Diary	Cuinchy	08/03/1915	12/03/1915
War Diary	Bethune	13/03/1915	20/03/1915
War Diary	Annequin and Cuinchy	21/03/1915	25/03/1915
War Diary	Cuinchy Bethune	26/03/1915	31/03/1915
Miscellaneous	A Form. Messages And Signals.		
Operation(al) Order(s)	6th Bde Operation Order No. 10 By Brigadier General R. Fanshawe C.B., DSO, Appx. 2		
Map	Maps		
Miscellaneous	Attack Order March 10th Commanding		
Operation(al) Order(s)	6th Brigade Operation Order No. 11	09/03/1915	09/03/1915
Miscellaneous	C Form (Original). Messages And Signals.		
Miscellaneous	C Form (Duplicate). Messages And Signals.		
Miscellaneous	A Form. Messages And Signals.		
Heading	2nd Division 6th Inf. Bde War Diary 5th Battalion Liverpool Regiment April 1915		
War Diary	Bethune	01/04/1915	04/04/1915
War Diary	Bethune & Cuinchy	05/04/1915	06/04/1915
War Diary	Vendin	07/04/1915	08/04/1915
War Diary	Bethune	09/04/1915	10/04/1915
War Diary	Cuinchy & Vicinity	11/04/1915	16/04/1915
War Diary	Annequin & Bethune	17/04/1915	20/04/1915
War Diary	Cuinchy & Vicinity	21/04/1915	24/04/1915
War Diary	Cuinchy & Vicinity & Bethune.	25/04/1915	28/04/1915
War Diary	Cuinchy & Vicinity	29/04/1915	30/04/1915
Heading	6th Infantry Brigade 2nd Division War Diary 5th Battn. The King's (Liverpool Regiment). May 1915		
War Diary	Cuinchy	01/05/1915	02/05/1915
War Diary	Bethune.	03/05/1915	08/05/1915
War Diary	Le Touret & Richebourg St Vaast	09/05/1915	09/05/1915
War Diary	Richebourg St. Vaast	09/05/1915	10/05/1915
War Diary	Le Touret.	11/05/1915	14/05/1915
War Diary	Le Touret & Vicinity Richebourg.	15/05/1915	15/05/1915
War Diary	Richebourg	16/05/1915	18/05/1915
War Diary	Le Touret	19/05/1915	19/05/1915
War Diary	Vendin	20/05/1915	20/05/1915
War Diary	Lozinghem	21/05/1915	30/05/1915

War Diary	Maroc.	31/05/1915	31/05/1915
Miscellaneous	Notes on Holding "W" Section.		
Miscellaneous	Notes on holding "W" Section.	21/05/1915	21/05/1915
Heading	6th Infantry Brigade, 2nd Division, War Diary 5th Battn. The King's (Liverpool Regiment). June 1915		
War Diary	Maroc	01/06/1915	04/06/1915
War Diary	Les Brebis	05/06/1915	05/06/1915
War Diary	Maroc	05/06/1915	06/06/1915
War Diary	Noeux Les Mines.	07/06/1915	10/06/1915
War Diary	Vermelles	11/06/1915	15/06/1915
War Diary	Fauqvereuil	16/06/1915	18/06/1915
War Diary	Annequin	19/06/1915	21/06/1915
War Diary	Cuinchy	22/06/1915	26/06/1915
War Diary	Tourbieres And Vicinity	27/06/1915	29/06/1915
War Diary	Cuinchy	30/06/1915	30/06/1915
Heading	6th Infantry Brigade, 2nd Division, War Diary 5th Battn. The King's (Liverpool Regiment). July 1915		
War Diary	Cuinchy	01/07/1915	05/07/1915
War Diary	Bethune	06/07/1915	13/07/1915
War Diary	Le Preol	14/07/1915	16/07/1915
War Diary	Guivenchy	17/07/1915	21/07/1915
War Diary	Bethune & Le Preol	22/07/1915	22/07/1915
War Diary	Le Preol	23/07/1915	25/07/1915
War Diary	Guivenchy	26/07/1915	29/07/1915
War Diary	Vendin	30/07/1915	31/07/1915
Heading	6th Infantry Brigade. 2nd Division. War Diary 5th Battn. The King's (Liverpool Regiment). August 1915		
War Diary	Vendin	01/08/1915	03/08/1915
War Diary	Beuvry	04/08/1915	12/08/1915
War Diary	Beuvry & Cuinchy	13/08/1915	17/08/1915
War Diary	Beuvry	18/08/1915	30/08/1915
Miscellaneous	Appendices 4,5,6,7		
Miscellaneous	Officer Commanding Appx. 6	18/08/1915	18/08/1915
Miscellaneous	A Form. Messages And Signals. Appx 7		
Miscellaneous	A Form. Messages And Signals. Appx 4		
Miscellaneous	A Form. Messages And Signals. Appx 5		
Heading	6th Infantry Brigade. 2nd Division War Diary 5th Battn. The King's (Liverpool Regiment). September 1915		
War Diary	Beuvry	01/09/1915	07/09/1915
War Diary	Cuinchy	08/09/1915	12/09/1915
War Diary	Annequin & Vicinity	13/09/1915	16/09/1915
War Diary	Bethune & Cuinchy Etc.	16/09/1915	20/09/1915
War Diary	Bethune	21/09/1915	24/09/1915
War Diary	Govre & Le Quesnoy	25/09/1915	26/09/1915
War Diary	Cambrin & Cuinchy	27/09/1915	30/09/1915
Heading	6th Infantry Brigade. 2nd Division. War Diary 5th Battn. The King's (Liverpool Regiment). October 1915		
War Diary	Bethune.	01/10/1915	01/10/1915
War Diary	Vermelles Vicinity near TM Dump	02/10/1915	02/10/1915
War Diary	Vermelles & Vicinity The Dump	03/10/1915	03/10/1915
War Diary	Bethune	04/10/1915	08/10/1915
War Diary	Le Quesnoy	09/10/1915	10/10/1915
War Diary	Bethune	11/10/1915	21/10/1915
War Diary	Cuinchy	22/10/1915	24/10/1915
War Diary	Annequin	25/10/1915	27/10/1915
War Diary	Cuinchy	27/10/1915	31/10/1915

Heading	6th Infantry Brigade. 2nd Division. War Diary 5th Battn. The King's (Liverpool Regiment). November 1915		
War Diary	Cuinchy	01/11/1915	02/11/1915
War Diary	Beuvry	03/11/1915	04/11/1915
War Diary	Busnettes	05/11/1915	05/11/1915
War Diary	Cuinchy	01/11/1915	02/11/1915
War Diary	Beuvry	03/11/1915	04/11/1915
War Diary	Busnettes	05/11/1915	12/11/1915
War Diary	Bethune	13/11/1915	13/11/1915
War Diary	Vermelles Trenches	14/11/1915	14/11/1915
War Diary	Vermelles	15/11/1915	18/11/1915
War Diary	Vermelles Trenches	19/11/1915	20/11/1915
War Diary	Beuvry	20/11/1915	22/11/1915
War Diary	Vermelles Trenches	23/11/1915	25/11/1915
War Diary	Beuvry	26/11/1915	29/11/1915
War Diary	Cambrin Trenches	30/11/1915	30/11/1915
Heading	6th Infantry Brigade. 2nd Division. 5th Battn. The King's (Liverpool Regiment). December 1915		
War Diary	Cambrin	01/12/1915	04/12/1915
War Diary	Beuvry	05/12/1915	06/12/1915
War Diary	Cambrin	07/12/1915	10/12/1915
War Diary	Beuvry	11/12/1915	12/12/1915
War Diary	Cambrin	13/12/1915	17/12/1915
War Diary	Annequin S.	18/12/1915	19/12/1915
War Diary	Cambrin	20/12/1915	23/12/1915
War Diary	Annequin S.	24/12/1915	25/12/1915
War Diary	Cambrin.	26/12/1915	31/12/1915
Heading	Patrol Report 21.12.15.		
Miscellaneous	Patrol Report.		

WO 95/13690 (3)

2nd Division

War Diaries

5th Battn Liverpool Regt. joined 24-2-15,

From 1st February. To 31st December 1915

To 55 Div Jan 1916
165 BDE

2nd Division
6th Inf. Bde.

Battalion disembarked at Havre from
United Kingdom on February 22nd 1915.

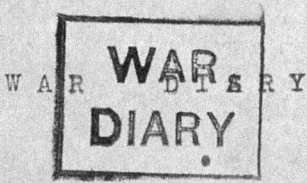

5th Battalion LIVERPOOL REGIMENT

February

1 9 1 5

Army Form C. 2118.

WAR DIARY
or
INTELLIGENCE SUMMARY.
(Erase heading not required.)

Place	Date	Hour	Summary of Events and Information	Remarks and references to Appendices
Canterbury	Feb/15			
	1		Bn. + Coy Training & Musketry.	G.S.B.
	2		Bn. & Coy. Training & Musketry.	G.S.B.
	3		Bn. & Coy. Training & Musketry.	G.S.B.
	4		Bn. & Coy. Training & Musketry.	G.S.B.
	5		Bn. & Coy. Training & Musketry.	G.S.B.
	6		Transport replaced by new issue	G.S.B.
			Bn. & Coy. Training & Musketry.	
	7		Church Parade.	G.S.B.
	8		Bn. & Coy. Training & Musketry.	G.S.B.
	9		Bn. & Coy. Training & Musketry.	G.S.B.
	10		Bn. & Coy. Training & Musketry.	G.S.B.
	11		Inspection of Bn. by Earl of Derby K.G.	G.S.B.
			Bn. & Coy Training & Musketry.	

Army Form C. 2118.

WAR DIARY
or
INTELLIGENCE SUMMARY.

(Erase heading not required.)

Instructions regarding War Diaries and Intelligence Summaries are contained in F. S. Regs., Part II. and the Staff Manual respectively. Title pages will be prepared in manuscript.

Place	Date Feb/15	Hour	Summary of Events and Information	Remarks and references to Appendices
Canterbury	12		Bn. & Co. Training	C.R.B.
	13		Inspection of Transport of Bn. by D. of T.	C.R.B.
	13		Bn. & Co. Training.	C.R.B.
	14		Church Parade.	C.R.B.
	15		Bn. & Co. Training.	C.R.B.
	16		Bn. & Co. Training.	C.R.B.
	17		Bn. & Co. Training. Issue of new Equipment.	C.R.B.
	18		Inspection of Bn. by Brigadier. Equipping the Bn.	C.R.B.
	19		Equipping the Bn. Issue of Mark VII Amm.	C.R.B.
	20	4.45 p.m.	Equipping of Bn. completed. Orders received to leave Canterbury to-morrow morning in three trains at 6.55 A.M. 8.25 A.M. & 10 A.M.	C.R.B.

WAR DIARY
or
INTELLIGENCE SUMMARY.

(Erase heading not required.)

Army Form C. 2118.

Place	Date Feb/15	Hour	Summary of Events and Information	Remarks and references to Appendices
Canterbury.	21.		Left Canterbury & duly detrained at Southampton where the Bn. embarked in H.M. Transport of Argyle & "Queen Empress". The transport was embarked separately on "Manchester Importer." Strength of Bn. — Officers 31. Other ranks 1100. Sailed at 5.20 P.M. and arrived at Havre 12 midnight.	E.R.B.
Havre.	22		Disembarked at Havre at 8 A.M. and marched to Rest Camp No. I. at St Adresse where the Bn. was accomodated under canvas. Fur coats were issued & all necessaries & clothing made up.	E.R.B.
Havre.	23		Marched to Havre Railway Station & entrained. Left Havre 4.45 P.M. for destination unknown.	E.R.B.
Bethune.	24.	2 P.M.	Arrived at Bethune, detrained, & marched to the French Barracks for the night. Officers were billeted in the Town. Received orders to move to Vendin-lez-Bethune to-morrow.	E.R.B.
Bethune.	25.		We learn that we became part of the VI Infantry Brigade commanded by Brigadier General R. Fanshawe C.B. D.S.O. which forms part	

Army Form C. 2118.

WAR DIARY
or
INTELLIGENCE SUMMARY.
(Erase heading not required.)

Instructions regarding War Diaries and Intelligence Summaries are contained in F. S. Regs., Part II and the Staff Manual respectively. Title pages will be prepared in manuscript.

Place	Date	Hour	Summary of Events and Information	Remarks and references to Appendices
Bethune.	25.		of II Division of 1st Army.	
		2. P.M.	Gen. Horne comdg. II Division inspected the Bn.; after which, the Bn. proceeded by march route to Vendin-lez-Bethune then to go into billets. Arrived at 4 P.M. less B. Coy. which was attached to the 1 K.R.R. for a 4 shortens of duty of instruction in trenches at Guinchy.	G.S.R.
Vendin-lez-Bethune.	26th.		Company training.	G.S.R.
"	27th.		Company training. C. O. relieved B with 1/K.R.R.	G.S.R.
"	28.		Company training. C. O. Adj: & M. O. inspected trenches.	G.S.R.

2nd Division
6th Inf. Bde.

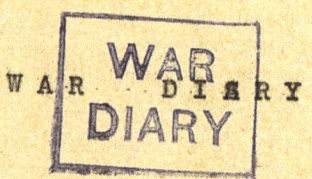

5th Battalion LIVERPOOL REGIMENT

March

1 9 1 5

Attached:- Appendices 1 & 2.

Army Form C. 2118.

WAR DIARY
or
INTELLIGENCE SUMMARY.
(Erase heading not required.)

Place	Date	Hour	Summary of Events and Information	Remarks and references to Appendices
Vendin-ley - Bethune.	Mar/15 1st.		Company training. D.Co. relieved C. in trenches. Orders received to proceed to-morrow by march route to billets in vicinity of Pont Tournant. A & B Co. & 2a Barrée Canal. 1500 x E. of Bethune.	S/B C.S.B.
Vendin-ley - Bethune	2.		Left Vendin - ley - Bethune 10.45 A.M. less D.Co. less D.Co. and C.Co. (C.C. remained in old billets) and arrived at Pont Tournant - 12 mid day. 1st Reinforcement under 2/Lt. Russell joined the Bn. from Rouen. Nos 5 & 6 Platoon attached to S. Staffs R. for trench duty.	C.S.B.
Pont-Tournant	3.		Received orders to stand by & be prepared for a run at short notice, as a German attack was rumoured again. South of La Barrée Canal. A Co. relieved D in trenches.	S.S.B

1577 Wt.W10791/1773 500,000 1/15 D.D.&L. A.D.S.S./Forms/C.2118.

Army Form C. 2118.

WAR DIARY
or
INTELLIGENCE SUMMARY.
(Erase heading not required.)

Instructions regarding War Diaries and Intelligence Summaries are contained in F. S. Regs., Part II. and the Staff Manual respectively. Title pages will be prepared in manuscript.

Place	Date	Hour	Summary of Events and Information	Remarks and references to Appendices
Pont Tournant	Mar/15. 4		Instruction in trench duties.	C.S.R.
	5		Instruction in field duties	C.S.R.
	6		Instruction in trench duties.	C.S.R.
	7		Church Parade. Instruction in trench duties. Instruction in use of hand grenades. Received order to move to - move to Cuinchy.	C.S.R.
	8		Left Pont Tournant & arrived at Cuinchy at 12 mid-day. Bn. is now distributed as follows. Bn. Head Quarters & No 9 & 11 Platoons at Cuinchy. B. & D. Coys under command of Maj Shute at Cuinchy to form part
Cuinchy			of Sec. B. III viz. 1 K.R.R. Section.

1577 Wt.W10791/1773 500,000 1/15 D.D. & L. A.D.S.S./Forms/C. 2118.

WAR DIARY or INTELLIGENCE SUMMARY

Army Form 2118.

(Erase heading not required.)

Instructions regarding War Diaries and Intelligence Summaries are contained in F.S. Regs., Part II. and the Staff Manual respectively. Title pages will be prepared in manuscript.

Place	Date Mar.	Hour	Summary of Events and Information	Remarks and references to Appendices
Cuinchy	8th		Continued –	
			Nos. 10 & 12 Platoons allotted to Sec. B. II wing the section held by 1 L/mal R. & Berks. R.	5/8
			A. Co. allotted to Sec. B. I. wing the section of line held by S. Staff at Cuinchy.	eseb.
			Bn. transport at Le Quesnoy.	
			Duty in trenches.	
	9th		In evening orders were received to attack the German position on morning of 10th by VI Inf. Bde.	eseb.
	10th		Assault by VI Infantry Brigade of enemy position in vicinity of Cuinchy and Givenchy took place. Dispositions of Battalion as follows. R.h. Head Quarters and ½ C. Coy. Garrison for Pont Fixe and Sidney Defences. ½ C. Coy. with Centre Column. Comdr. Lt. Col. Carter 1/K. R.'s. Garrison for enemy line; A. Co. with Right Column. Comdr. Lt. Col. Routledge 2/S. Staffs. Garrison	BATTLE of NEUVE CHAPELLE

WAR DIARY
or
INTELLIGENCE SUMMARY.

Army Form C. 2118.

Place	Date	Hour	Summary of Events and Information	Remarks and references to Appendices
	Mar 10	Continued		
			...our enemy fire.	
			B and C Coys with Left Column. Contr. Maj Shackerley 1/K.R.R. Garrison of Machine Guns with Left Column employed enemy fire.	
		7 a.m.	Artillery commenced replying on enemy line.	
		7.30 a.m.	2nd Artillery bombardment commenced.	
		7.40 a.m.	Ceased.	
		7.50 a.m.	Second Artillery bombardment commenced of this church became very intense.	
		8.10 a.m.	Infantry delivered the assault, heavy machine gun and infantry fire coming to the enemy lashed our remaining front till attack. The assault was not successful, though him after him first had in marked forward to the assault in face of a terrific gun and infantry fire from the enemy and hanging the enemy wire was intact all the time. This was our first baptism of fire and all ranks behaved in an exemplary manner. The whole advance under a very heavy fire, & an absolute disregard of personal danger.	

The Commanding Officer of B and A Coys, was Major J.J. SHUTE attached to 1/K.R.R.

March 10th continued

WAR DIARY or INTELLIGENCE SUMMARY

Army Form C.2118.

Place	Date	Hour	Summary of Events and Information	Remarks and references to Appendices
	10th		was especially commended by the Officer Comdg. 1/K.R.R. The company in support – viz. B & D Cos. who were entrenched to hold the front line until further orders. This was done during evening and night. March 10/11. Good work was done in individual cases of helping the wounded and fetching same whilst to Field Ambulance waiting to be taken to Field Ambulance. One casualty was Orne ranks four killed, and nineteen wounded, one of whom died from his wounds. Copy of message from General Sir Charles Munro, also of orders and sketch – vide Appendix.	APPX 1. APPX 2.
		5 pm	O.C. 1/K.R.R.	

WAR DIARY
or
INTELLIGENCE SUMMARY
(Erase heading not required).

Army Form C.2118.

Instructions regarding War Diaries and Intelligence Summaries are contained in F.S. Regs., Part II and the Staff Manual respectively. Title Pages will be prepared in manuscript.

Place.	Date Nov/15	Hour	Summary of Events and Information.	Remarks and references to Appendices
CUINCHY.	11.		The enemy heavily bombarded but no further amount left here.	C.S.R.
"	12.		Further bombardment of enemy. The II Inf. Bde. was relieved by the IV Guards Bde on 12th. inst. in BETHUNE & COLLEGE de JEUNES FILLES.	C.S.R.
BETHUNE.	13.		Rested and cleaned up generally.	C.S.R.
"	14.		Church Parade.	C.S.R.
"	15.		Company training carried on.	C.S.R.
"	16.		Company training carried on.	C.S.R.
"	17.		Company training carried on.	C.S.R.
"	18.		Company training carried on.	C.S.R.

Army Form C. 2118.

WAR DIARY
or
INTELLIGENCE SUMMARY.
(Erase heading not required.)

Instructions regarding War Diaries and Intelligence Summaries are contained in F. S. Regs., Part II. and the Staff Manual respectively. Title pages will be prepared in manuscript.

Place	Date Mar/15	Hour	Summary of Events and Information	Remarks and references to Appendices
Paturent	19.		Company training carried out.	G.R.S.
"	20.		Company training carried out.	G.R.S.
"	21.		On Battn. move on Fouquereuil — H.Q. and B. Co. to Annequin. A. & C. Co. to Cuinchy huts. S. branch of Canal. Fatigues & training work.	
Annequin Cuinchy			D. Co. to Cuinchy Supporting Point. Beuvry. Branch duty.	G.R.S.
"	22.		Branch duty.	G.R.S.
"	23.		B. Co. relieved D at Cuinchy Supporting Point. Branch duty. Following casualties:— No. 2745 McKenzie and No. 2678 Rfn. Hepworth were killed; and 2/Lieut. MacDonald wounded.	G.R.S.
"	24.		Branch duty. Following casualties:— One Officer (Lieut. Arkwright) and four men wounded.	G.R.S.
"	25.		Following move:— Bn H.Q. to Cuinchy Supporting Point. D. Co. to huts etc. A. & C. Co. under Maj Shute proceed to Lillie et Béthune.	G.R.S.

WAR DIARY
or
INTELLIGENCE SUMMARY.
(Erase heading not required.)

Instructions regarding War Diaries and Intelligence Summaries are contained in F. S. Regs., Part II. and the Staff Manual respectively. Title pages will be prepared in manuscript.

Place	Date March	Hour	Summary of Events and Information	Remarks and references to Appendices
Cuinchy & Bethune	26		Trench duty. Bn. H.2. B and D Coys. Rest & clean up. A & C Coys.	G.R.O.
Cuinchy & Bethune	27		Trench duty. Bn. H.2. B and D Coys. Company training. A & C Coys.	G.R.O. G.S.O.
			Three men wounded.	
Cuinchy & Bethune	28		A. & C. Coy relieve B & D Coy. Un lent his rammed procedd to Bethune.	G.R.O.
			Trench duty.	
			Two men wounded.	
Cuinchy & Bethune	29		Trench duty. B & D Coy clean up & rest.	G.R.O.
			Two men wounded.	
Cuinchy & Bethune	30		Trench duty. Company training.	G.R.O.
Cuinchy & Bethune	31		Trench duty. Company training. One man wounded.	G.R.O.

"A" Form.   Army Form C. 2121.
MESSAGES AND SIGNALS.   No. of Message _____

APPX 1

| TO | 1/5 King's |

Sender's Number	Day of Month	In reply to Number	AAA
B.M. 169	TENTH		

Following from General Sir Charles MUNRO AAA I feel confident the bravery and stedfastness of the 6th Bde was today what it has always been ever since I have known them AAA The GOC 2nd Division adds that when the 6th Bde do not succeed no other troops can AAA They have made a great effort.

Copy to Capt P. Bt. Major
Bde Major 6th Bde.

From: 6th Bde
Place:
Time: 8·45 pm

SECRET   APPX. 2.   Copy No 10

6th Bde Operation Order No 10
by Brigadier General R. Fanshawe, C.B., DSO.

1. (a) **PLAN** The brigade, supported by other troops, will attack the German trenches.

(b) **OBJECTIVE.** The objective will be the trench A1, B1, C1, D1, E1, E3 (vide attached sketch) together with the trench just to rear of it, viz A2, B2, C2, D2, E2, E4.

The battle line will be given to the troops as the objective in one bound from our trenches.

(c) **Distribution of Troops**

Columns / Commander	Assaulting troops	Garrison for Covering fire	Reel	Route	Objective
Right Lt. Col Routledge 2/S. Staffs	2 Sections E. Anglian Fd. Coy 3 coys S. Staffs 2 machine guns	1 coy S. Staffs 1 coy 5th L'pools 4 machine guns — Front covered L – M – O		ORCHARD FM – GIVENCHY road trench – MAIRIE redoubt – LOOKOUT – LORGIES road trench – and all ground South and East of it.	German trench near B1 and B2 pushing left till meeting centre column.
Centre Lt. Col CARTER 1st Kings	1 Section 5th Fd. Co. 3 coys 1st Kings 2 machine guns	1 coy 1/Kings ½ coy 5th L'pools 4 machine guns — Front covered O – P – Q		Communications in B2 lines thrown above as allotted to right column.	German trench from NE corner of ORCHARD to near C1, pushing to right to meet right column near LORGIES road & getting touch with left column near NE corner of ORCHARD
LEFT Major SHAKERLEY 1/KRR	1 Section 5th Fd. Co. 3 coys KRR 2 machine guns 1 Coy KRR	1 coy KRR 2 coy 5th L'pools 4 machine guns — Front covered R – S – T		Communications as in B3	German trench E1 to E3 pushing to right to get touch with centre column near NE corner of ORCHARD

The rear limit of the assaulting columns will be ORCHARD FARM – GIVENCHY ROAD trench – MAIRIE redoubt – KEEP – MOAT HOUSE

Brigade Reserve

     3 sections 5th Field Coy   W. of Keep
     ~~2 Platoons 5th Liverpools~~
     2 sections East Anglian Fd Co. PONT FIXE
     H.Q. and ~~coys 5th Liverpools~~ — PONT FIXE and SIDBURY dugouts
     ½ Coy 5th/Liverpools

Brigade Reserve (contd)

~~1 Batt~~

1 Battn Royal Berks — Under cover in area SIDBURY — W of KEEP – WINDY CORNER

2 mountain guns   1 FRENCH FARM
1 SIDBURY

2. **General Details**

(a) Troops when halted will clear the main communication trenches and stay in the siding cover trenches till required to advance. During the advance the front line as it is vacated will be kept filled from the rear.

(b) About 200 shovels and some picks will be stored ready for issue on each column's line of advance well forward, & when required carried forward by parties of men.

(c) Every man will carry two empty sandbags

(d) 170 rounds of ammunition per man will be carried, & a battalion reserve of 10 boxes stored near the shovels, with a reserve of bombs or grenades also

A brigade reserve of ammunition, bombs & tools will be established just north of the KEEP on the road

About 50 bombs should be carried for each trench to be bombed viz the two main trenches to each flank of each column, & the 3 or 4 communication trenches leading EAST

(e) The OC the sections of each Field Co. will tell off blocking parties of 4 sappers for each trench to be blocked.

(f) The assaulting column will not wear packs & these and any other surplus gear will be temporarily stored by companies in a convenient place as all dug outs & cover will be used by other troops as they advance.

3. Casualties will be brought to Advanced Collecting Stations near KEEP & on ORCHARD Farm road, by regimental Stretcher Bearers & thence to the present Dressing Stations on the PONT FIXE – WINDY CORNER Road by the Field Ambulance Bearer Division

4. Attention is called to the copy of secret notes issued to Bns. on 5th inst. Hours for troops to be in position & details of covering fire will be issued later, with date for operations.

5. Reports to Brigade Head Quarters.

Attack Orders
March 10th
Cannonenburg

6th Brigade Operation Order No: 11

Copy No. 7

9th, March, 1915.

1. The operations projected in Brigade Operation Order No: 10. of the 6th instant will be carried out tomorrow, the 10th instant.

(a) Preliminary Movements.

2. The following time-table will be adhered to:—
All troops (except the rear companies of 1st R. Berks) are to be in position by 7.30 a.m.
The 1st R. Berks. will ensure clearing CANAL JUNCTION by 6.50 a.m. and will march straight to their allotted position.

(b) Covering Fire Artillery.

7 a.m. Artillery commence registering on enemy wire. Trenches opposite the points to be registered on will be very thinly held, and such men as are left in the trenches should be instructed to keep well down.

7.30 a.m. First Artillery Bombardment commences. Places in the trenches which will be dangerous for our troops should be cleared by this hour.

7.40 a.m. First Artillery Bombardment ceases.

7.50 a.m. Second Artillery Bombardment commences.

8.5 a.m. Artillery Bombardment becomes "intense."

8.10 a.m. (a). Artillery lengthens on to trenches further back and to the flanks.
(b). Infantry deliver the assault.

(c) Covering Fire Infantry

7.38 a.m. The Infantry and Machine Guns of garrisons along our front open a heavy fire to continue for three minutes and ceasing one minute after close of first Artillery Bombardment.

8.7 a.m. Infantry and Machine Guns again open heavy fire, to be maintained during the remainder of bombardment and becoming very intense while our assaulting parties are rushing forward.

3. The left column having now been allotted two companies 5th Liverpools instead of one the Brigade Reserve will be composed and distributed

3 (continued).

distributed as under:-

Brigade Reserve.

1 Section 5th Fd. Coy. R.E.	West of KEEP.
1 Section 5th Fd. Coy. R.E.	Dug Outs just East of Brigade Hd. Qrs.
2 Sections East Anglian Fd. Coy. R.E.	Houses in GIVENCHY - ORCHARD FARM Road
Hd. Qrs. and ½ Coy. 5th Liverpools	PONT FIXE and SIDBURY defences.
1st Bn. Royal Berks.	Under cover in area SIDBURY - West of KEEP - WINDY CORNER.
2 Mountain Guns.	FRENCH FARM.

2 sections to Porte Bank by 7-30 A.M.

4. A bearer sub-division 6th Field Ambulance will be at the King's old dressing station in the PONT-FIXE - WINDY CORNER Road from 7.15 a.m.

5. Watches will be set at Brigade Head Quarters at 5.30 p.m. this evening.

6. Reports as previously directed.

Uhlley, Br. Major
Brigade Major 6th Infantry Bde.

Issued at 5.30 p.m.

"C" Form (Original). Army Form C. 2123.

MESSAGES AND SIGNALS.   No. of Message

Prefix	Code	Words	Received	Sent, or sent out	Office Stamp
		£ s. d.	From	At 5 m.	Liverpool
Charges to collect			By	To	
Service Instructions				By	

Handed in at the _____ Office, at _____ .m. Received here at _____ .m.

TO   6th Batt Ordrs

Sender's Number.	Day of Month.	In reply to Number.	AAA
M 16/	15th		

1) The following redistribution of the 6th Batt line will be carried out tonight.

(a) A Battalion 4th Hy A.A. will take over the line now held by the 1/Kings, & also that part of the line held by the 1/Staffords up to such as the junction of the trenches with the Northern arm of the WILLOW ROAD BEND.

(b) The 1/Staffords will continue the line SOUTH to the CANAL.

(c) The 1/K.R.R. will continue to hold their present line.

(d) The 1/Rhodes will remain in the area SIDBURY - WEST OF KEEP - WINDY CORNER.

FROM
PLACE
TIME

* This line should be erased if not required.
278259—W. 60—W. & S. Ltd.—(E)—30,000 Pads.—4-12.

"C" Form (Original). Army Form C. 2123.
MESSAGES AND SIGNALS. No. of Message_____

Prefix Code Words	Received	Sent, or sent out	Office Stamp.
£ s. d.	From	At _____ m.	
Charges to collect	By	To	
Service Instructions.		By	

Handed in at the _____ Office, at _____ m. Received here at _____ m.

TO

Sender's Number.	Day of Month.	In reply to Number.

AAA

e) The 1/Kings, after relief, will move into Brigade Reserve in dugouts ~~east~~ WEST of PONT FIXE – WINDY CORNER Road.

f) That portion of the 1/S Staffords who are to be relieved by the Guards Battalion will return to PONT FIXE Billets.

g) Relief of 1/Kings & part of S/Staffs will be mutually arranged on arrival of Officers of the Guards Battalion concerned.

h) The detachment of the S/Staffs now attached to R.F.R. & 1/S Staffs will rejoin their own units. Also the 2 platoons now attached to 1/Kings will rejoin their own H.Q at PONT FIXE.

FROM
PLACE
TIME

i) Batt H.Q. will return for the night to ~~house~~ the spot formerly occupied.

5.30 pm

*This line should be erased if not required.
278259—W. 60—W. & S. Ltd.—(E)—30,000 Pads.—4-12.

Rec'd 8.45 pm 9/11/14

"C" Form (Duplicate). Army Form C. 2123.
MESSAGES AND SIGNALS. No. of Message..........

| Service Instructions. | Charges to Pay. £ s. d. | Office Stamp. 10-3-15 |

Handed in at **XF** Office **2.45** m. Received **2.46** m.

TO **5TH Liverpools**

| Sender's Number | Day of Month | In reply to Number | |
| BM 147 | 10TH | | AAA |

Fresh assault is taking place at 2.45 pm

Please initial

FROM **6TH Bde**
PLACE & TIME **2.48 PM**

"A" Form. Army Form C. 2121.
MESSAGES AND SIGNALS.

TO: 1/5. Kings

Sender's Number: VI:53 Day of Month: TENTH AAA

Following from General Sir D. HAIG begins the field marshal Commdg in Chief wishes his heartiest congratulations to be conveyed to corps commanders and all ranks of 1st Army for the splendid success which they have gained today AAA Would you also kindly express my gratitude for the magnificent determination which you and all ranks have displayed in executing my orders issued for todays battle AAA The enemy has been completely surprised and I trust that tomorrow the effect of todays fighting will result in still further successes AAA Ends.

From: 9th Bde
Place: Bde Major City Junction
Time: 10.30 pm

"A" Form. Army

MESSAGES AND SIGNALS.

APPX 2

TO: Batts — Irish Guards — Staffs. Rifles
On wings — 5th R'guts

Sender's Number: Bm 225
Day of Month: 11th

Re my started	Bm 219 about	SECOND 12	STAGE noon	

From: 8th Rifle
Place:
Time: 12.25 pm

"A" Form.   Army Form C. 212.

MESSAGES AND SIGNALS.

TO: 1/5 King's
— 6th. Brigade Orders.

Sender's Number: B.M. 199
Day of Month: Eleventh
AAA

1. 6th Bde will resume offensive to-day AAA First stage deliberate attempt by Artillery to knock out N.E. Corner of ORCHARD and to establish in two places S.E. of that point commencing at 8 a.m.

2. K.R.R., Irish Guards and Staffords will open covering and rifle and machine gun fire at that hour.

3. The 1st R Berks will be in readiness from 7.30 a.m. to push in against the point bombarded AAA The Officers Commanding K.R.R. and Irish Guards will mutually arrange as to the length of trenches to be left clear by Guards for Berks to mass in and also for clearing the Berks lines of approach.

4. YKRR and 2/ Staffs will keep 1 Coy. each of their local Reserves in utmost readiness to support Berks if required.

From:
Place:
Time:

The above may be forwarded as now corrected. (Z)

"A" Form. Army Form C.2.
MESSAGES AND SIGNALS. No. of Message_____

Prefix___ Code___ m.	Words.	Charge.	This message is on a/c of:	Recd. at___ (2) m.
Office of Origin and Service Instructions.	Sent			Date___
	At___ m.		_____Service.	From___
	To___			
	By___		(Signature of "Franking Officer.")	By___

TO {

Sender's Number	Day of Month	In reply to Number	A A A
* BM. 199	11th		

5/ 1 Sec. 5th 2nd Co. R.E. will be attached to 4/Berks for the day.

6/ Irish Guards will arrange to clear during the bombardment such trenches as the artillery wish emptied

7/ 4KRR will detail one of their 2 Coys 5th Liverpools also to be in instant readiness to support 4/Berks.

8/ The 3 Coys detailed for instant readiness will be kept under cover in their respective areas AAA Remaining troops will be in Brigade Reserve and will remain in readiness in their billets.

9/ The Communication trenches ORCHARD FARM — GIVENCHY and KEEP — MAIRIE REDOUBT — LOOKOUT are to be kept clear of troops for free advancement.

10/ Reports to Bde Hd Qrs.

From_____
Place_____
Time 6.50 A.M.

The above may be forwarded as now corrected. (Z) Tchll, B.Major

Censor. Signature of Addressor or person authorised to telegraph in his name

* This line should be erased if not required.

"A" Form.
Army Form C.21...

MESSAGES AND SIGNALS.

No. of Message _____

Prefix ____ Code ____ m. | Words. | Charge. | This message is on a/c of: | Recd. at ____ m.
Office of Origin and Service Instructions. | Sent | | | Date ____
| At ____ m. | | ____ Service. | From ____
| To ____ | | |
| By ____ | | (Signature of "Franking Officer.") | By ____

TO { 1/5 Kings

Sender's Number	Day of Month	In reply to Number	A A A
* B.M. 219	Eleventh		

Bombardment will be conducted in three stages AAA First stage now in progress to demolish N.E. Corner ORCHARD AAA Second Stage Howitzers will bombard from NE Corner ORCHARD to Barrier on LORGIES Road until artillery report wire broken up AAA Third stage slow fire will be maintained ending up with intense fire for ten minutes AAA Exact time for cessation of bombardment and infantry assaults will be notified to you about half an hour before being given AAA Portion of front of wood for assaulting parties should open covering fire from rifles and machine guns during last stage AAA Will notify you when last stage commences AAA Acknowledge.

From Col. Balls
Place Bde Major 6th ___ Bde
Time 10.30 a.m.

The above may be forwarded as now corrected. (Z)

Rec'd 11 A.M. 11-3-15 Acknowledged

2nd Division
6th Inf. Bde.

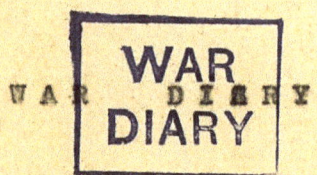

5th Battalion LIVERPOOL REGIMENT

April

1 9 1 5

WAR DIARY or INTELLIGENCE SUMMARY

Army Form C. 2118.

(Erase heading not required.)

Place	Date	Hour	Summary of Events and Information	Remarks and references to Appendices
Béthune	1 April		Bn. Hd. Qrs. A & C moved to billets at Béthune. Whole Bn. less M.G. Section now being in billets. No. 2798 Rfn. Gregg wounded & died of wounds same day. (see attached warnt.)	C.R.B.
"	2 April		General clean up. Company training.	C.R.B.
"	3.		Company training.	C.R.B.
"	4.		Divine Service.	C.R.B.
Béthune & Cuinchy	5.		Bn. H.Q., B & D Cos moved to billets at Cuinchy. A & C Cos remain Béthune under command of Maj Shirlie. Transport & Quartermaster Dept" are at Beuvry. M.G. Section – 2 Guns & detachments at Annequin.	C.R.B.
"	6		About 11.30 P.M. Germans exploded a mine immediately in front of our fire trench & one to our right – in front of the French position. – In each case they were from 20 to 30 yards short & did very little damage. This was followed by heavy rifle fire on both sides. No 22.40 2/Cpl Bonfield was killed and one man wounded.	
Vendin	7.		The whole Bn. go into billets at Vendin – les – Béthune less the M.G. Section.	C.R.B.
"	8.		Rest & clean up. Company training. M.G. Section rejoins the Bn.	C.R.B.
Béthune	9.		Bn. moved to billets at Béthune. C & D Coys. on S. bank remainder of Bn. on N. bank of M.G. Canal.	C.R.B.

Army Form C. 2118.

WAR DIARY
or
INTELLIGENCE SUMMARY.
(Erase heading not required.)

Instructions regarding War Diaries and Intelligence Summaries are contained in F. S. Regs., Part II. and the Staff Manual respectively. Title pages will be prepared in manuscript.

Place	Date 1915	Hour	Summary of Events and Information	Remarks and references to Appendices
Festubert	10 April		Company training.	L.S.B.
Givenchy & vicinity	11 April		Following moves took place :— Bttn to Givenchy trenches. A & C Co with Maj Shute to Givenchy Point. B. Co to Cambrin Supporting Point. D Co & Bn H.Q. to Annequin. M.G. Section to Loubières. Transport & Quarter master Dept. to Beuvry. A few rounds of shelling by the enemy — killed gun. of trench mortar — took place, and two other ranks were wounded.	C.S.B.
"	12 April		Trench duty & Company training. No 2 & 04 Rft. Wright — was killed.	L.S.B.
"	13 April		A. & C. Co with Maj Shute rejoined Bn H.Q. at Annequin on relief by 18 London Regt. D. Co relieved B. at Cambrin Supporting Point — B Co to Chay on D Co billets at Annequin.	L.S.B.
"	14 April		Shelled by enemy during early part of afternoon — his billets being hit. Two men were wounded.	L.S.B.

Army Form C. 2118.

WAR DIARY
or
INTELLIGENCE SUMMARY.
(Erase heading not required.)

Instructions regarding War Diaries and Intelligence Summaries are contained in F.S. Regs., Part II and the Staff Manual respectively. Title pages will be prepared in manuscript.

Place	Date 1915 April	Hour	Summary of Events and Information	Remarks and references to Appendices
Cuinchy & vicinity.	15.		The Battn. less D.G. remaining at Annequin - relieved 20th London Regt in the Cuinchy trenches. Guards duty.	6.2.R.
"	16.		Trench as follows:—	
Annequin & Bethune.	17		A. & C. Coys on relief by 7/8 Post R. to Bethune. B. Co. to Annequin. Bn. Head Quarters, Q.M. Dept. Transport to Bethune.	
			D.G. remain Annequin. M.G. Section to Bethune. — 2258 Sgt. Milne killed.	G.S.R.
			A.Co. moved to Annequin.	S.C.R.S.
	18.		Remainder of Bn. rejoin Bn. at Bethune.	Appx B
"	19.		Company training.	Appx C
"	20.		Trench as follows:— A. B. & D. Co to Cuinchy trenches: A Co spring to Cambrin Support Coint. C. Co. to Annequin.	
Cuinchy & vicinity	21		Bn. Hd Qrs to trenches. The enemy exploded a mine in front of the trench occupied by D.G. about 25 yards short though, but only one stone short of the head of our sapa. Seventeen men were wounded, Lt- anm killed. This mine made a large crater about 60ft long 40ft with 30ft deep & the earth was thrown up to 12 feet height absolutely blotting out view from a part of our	G.S.R.

Army Form C. 2118.

Page 2, of May 21.

WAR DIARY
or
INTELLIGENCE SUMMARY.
(Erase heading not required.)

5/8/15

Place	Date 1915 April	Hour	Summary of Events and Information	Remarks and references to Appendices
Cuinchy & vicinity.	22	night	During the night a great deal of bombing was carried on by both sides. The enemy heavily shelled the hill immediately on our right- occupied by 2/S. Staffs. who suffered some casualties. We had two men wounded.	G.S.B.
"	23		Enemy shelled out Supplying Point & we had one man wounded during the day.	G.S.B.
"	24		Trench duty continued. Very heavy men wounded, one of whom since died. Keel- who only rejoined us 2 days ago from a M.G. Course at St Omer. We were heavily shelled during the day & our artillery replied vigorously, doing considerable damage to the enemy.	G.S.B. G.S.B.
Cuinchy & vicinity & Bethune.	25		No 2 & 2 Pl'tns. two men wounded & died from their wounds. The Balln. (less A & C Cos & M.G. Section) on relief by 7/8 L'pool R proceeded to billets at Bethune – A & C Cos to Annequin. Part of M.G. Section to Annequin & part to touches – except Beaumont & 2.M. deft."	G.S.B.
"	26		A general rest & clean up.	G.S.B.
"	27		Company training. Demonstration in use of Bangalore torpedo.	G.S.B.
"	28		One NCO & ? Privates Wt. W14901/1272 50,000 1/15 D.D.& L.Ltd./ I.A.D.S.(F)/Forms/C.2118. Company training was carried out." proceeded to a M.G. Course at Wisques.	G.S.B.

Army Form C. 2118.

WAR DIARY
or
INTELLIGENCE SUMMARY.
(Erase heading not required.)

Places	Date	Hour	Summary of Events and Information	Remarks and references to Appendices
Cuinchy & vicinity.	1915 April 29.		Following morn:– A. Co. from Annequin to Cuinchy trenches. B.Q. from Betrune to Annequin. B.Q. :: Annequin to Cuinchy Supporting Point. D.Q. from Betrune to Cuinchy Supporting Point. Bn. Head Quarters from Betrune to Cuinchy Supporting Point.	
			2': Longhetton appointed Brigade bomb bombing Officer. No 741 Sgt Clarke was killed.	C.S.B.
	30.		Considerable bombing took place [& we had the following casualties:– No 2293 Cpl Roberts killed. No 2337 Rifn Lancastin wounded & died from wounds. 9 other men wounded.	C.S.B.
			In month – K. 7. W. 17 42	

6th Infantry Brigade.
2nd Division.

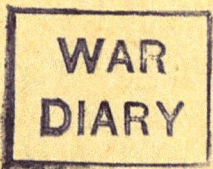

5th BATTN. THE KING'S (LIVERPOOL REGIMENT).

M A Y

1 9 1 5

Attached:

Notes on holding
"W" Section.

Army Form C. 2118.

WAR DIARY
or
INTELLIGENCE SUMMARY

(Erase heading not required.)

5/85 May 1915

Hour, Date, Place	Summary of Events and Information	Remarks and references to Appendices
Cuinchy 1st May 1915	Trench duty.	
	2．An night to Trench exploded a mine — result not known. 2/Lt C. Gill reported for duty after having been in hospital at Boulogne with a wound in the head. Casualties:— No 2527 Rfn Cavanagh killed and one man wounded.	C.R.B.
" 2nd May	Trench duty. Casualties:— Two men wounded.	C.R.B.
Bethune 3rd May.	The Battalion on relief by Glasgow Highlanders went into billets at Bethune. Casualties:— One man wounded.	C.R.B.
" 4th May	The Battalion had a general clean up and a rest.	C.R.B.
" 5th May.	Company training carried out.	
" 6th May.	Company training carried out.	C.R.B.
" 7th May.	Company training carried out. At 5 P.M. received orders to move at 1.49 AM 8th inst. Battn at mine for having been 24 hours.	C.R.B. C.R.B.

WAR DIARY or INTELLIGENCE SUMMARY

Army Form C. 2118.

Hour, Date, Place	Summary of Events and Information	Remarks and references to Appendices
Bethune. 8 May. Le Touret. 9th May. & Richebourg St Vaast	Company having carried out:- Bn. Battalion left 1.49 A.M. for Le Touret where Bn. arrived 3.15 A.M. At 5 a.m. our Artillery heavily bombarded enemy and at 5.40 a.m. the 1st Corps assaulted: the 1st Division carrying out assault, the 2nd Division, to which we belong, being in reserve. At 1 P.M. we got news, (mostly through wounded returning) that our 1st Division were being held up but that the 4th Corps on our left had broken the German line. At 3.20 P.M. our Artillery opened on intense fire on enemy and left an hour later the 1st Division again attacked but without success. At 4.15 P.M. our Brigade marched to Richebourg St Vaast - We arrived at 5.15 p.m. & waited in reserve for orders. At 6.30 P.M. received orders that Machine Gun Infantry Brigade would attack enemy breastworks	E.S.R.

Page 2 of May 9th.

WAR DIARY or INTELLIGENCE SUMMARY

Army Form C. 2118.

Hour, Date, Place	Summary of Events and Information	Remarks and references to Appendices
Richbourg St Vaast. 9 May 1915.	at 8.30 P.M. after an artillery bombardment commencing at 7.50 P.M. also to be prepared to move up to D line of trenches on receipt of orders. No further orders were received, & the Bn. remained in trenches occupying divided haven during the night. Intermittent firing took place all night.	
10 May.	At 6.30 a.m. orders received that XI Inf. Bde. will attack during the day - objective enemy front works near La Ferme Dessart du Bois & TIP after a few hours artillery bombardment commencing at 11 A.M. The 1/K.R.R. and 1/R. Berks will advance to the assault with ourselves in support. This attack was later on cancelled & the Bn. remained in trenches during the day. The following Officers employed the time to reconnoitre the position:- Lt. Col. Mahon & Adjt. Maj. Cohen. Capt. J.H. Chrisley and the M.G. Officer Lt. Billis. 5 P.M. received orders that XI Inf. Bde. would move to	S/H

WAR DIARY or INTELLIGENCE SUMMARY

Army Form C. 2118.

Part 2. 10th May 15.

Hour, Date, Place	Summary of Events and Information	Remarks and references to Appendices
RICHEBOURG ST VAAST.	Billets at LE TOURET and vicinity early next morning.	C.F.B.
LE TOURET. 11th May.	At 6.15 AM the Battalion fell in & moved off to billets near LE TOURET arriving there at 8.10 P.M. During the day the C.O., Adjutant, Captn Buckley and 2nd Lts made a careful reconnaissance of the trenches occupied by V Sgt Bde and of the enemy position. During this reconnaissance the enemy artillery were much in evidence.	
12 May.	A reconnaissance of the country North of RUE DU BOIS was made by Major Shute & Cohen, Captn Fairbrough, Worthorn Buckley and D.R. Brindley with the object of finding suitable bivouac ground and also lines of advance. During the night a practice night advance took place across country by a medium with the Bn: were	318 C.F.B

Page 2. 12th May.

WAR DIARY or INTELLIGENCE SUMMARY
Army Form C. 2118.

Hour, Date, Place	Summary of Events and Information	Remarks and references to Appendices
LE TOURET. May 12.	The 1/Kings and 2/8 Staffs. There were some very advanced dpln [depolyment] to be taught etc. and the ground selected afforded excellent practice in keeping touch with neighbouring troops.	G.S.B.
" 13	Moved to put billets about 1 mile S.W. in same vicinity	G.S.B.
" 14.	Orders were received that the VI Infantry Brigade would attack at 11.30 P.M. The 1/K.R.R. 2/R.Berks and 9/8 [?] Ryl R, who were in the trenches, when orders came from V Infantry Brigade, were to form the firing line & supports. The 1/8 [?] & 2/S. Staff and ourselves were to be Brigade Reserve. At 2.50 P.M. this order was cancelled.	G.S.B.

Army Form C. 2118

WAR DIARY
or
INTELLIGENCE SUMMARY.
(Erase heading not required.)

Hour, Date, Place	Summary of Events and Information	Remarks and references to Appendices
Le Touret & Vicinity Richebourg. 1st May/15.	Orders received that VI Inf. Bde. would attack the enemy Tuesday at 11.30 p.m. & that we were to furnish a working party of 2 Coys. for digging & intervening trenches of Battn. to be held in trenches near Richebourg. At 10.5 p.m. the Bn. marched out. "C" Richebourg, two Companies going to billets at Rue du Bois road in reserve, the remaining Coys. A. & B. and Bn. Hd. Qrs. moved on to Prince Albert road. This Coy. was placed at disposal of a R.E. Officer in front of the German front line trench & trench opposite after the attack on that to end to commence at 11.30 P.M. At the request of the R.E. another Platoon was sent for & duly arrived at Bn. Hd. Qrs. Everything in starting work occurred, caused as it afterwards transpired the R.E. Officer having been wounded. Several casualties through this period of working. Eventually a R.E. N.C.O. was sent to camp on with the working party. This party on leaving the trench came almost immediately under German rifle & M.G. fire and many casualties occurred, amongst them being Capt. W.E. Grubb & 2/Lieut G.F. Richardson of H.B. Coy. The working party was withdrawn just before dawn; having obeyed orders to withdraw at 2 A.M. finishing in the growing light; about 1.15. A.M. every available light, burning in the	R.S.B.

WAR DIARY
or
INTELLIGENCE SUMMARY.
(Erase heading not required.)

Army Form C. 2118.

Hour, Date, Place	Summary of Events and Information	Remarks and references to Appendices
RICHEBOURG. 16 May 1915.	About 4 a.m. C. & D. Coys. who had been brought up to the support trenches were ordered to advance into the firing line & support the 1st Bn. & pool in an attack on the German trenches. They moved to the fire trench with Bn. Hd. Qrs. across the open under heavy rifle & shell fire — both Adjutant of H.E. — Capt. J.H. GRINDLEY comdg. D. Co. & Capt. D.R GRINDLEY his second in command were both wounded during this advance; to former slightly, the latter severely. A. & B. Co. who had formed the night working party were already in the fire trench. The 1st Bn. had then delivered their attack & failed, suffering heavy loss. The O.C. 5 & L had been ordered to make a careful reconnaissance & report to G.O.C. Brigade on the situation. After reconnaissance & consultation with O.C. 1st L. had on left and O.C. 7th L. had on right, he reported that he considered assault was impracticable without incurring heavy losses. The Brigade ordered an attack to be made so at about 5 AM the 5 & 4 No 6. Platoon led the attack under Capt. W.L. EVANS	5/18 C.L.R.

WAR DIARY or INTELLIGENCE SUMMARY

Page 2 of 16th May. Army Form 2118.

Place	Date	Hour	Summary of Events and Information	Remarks and references to Appendices
RICHEBOURG	16th May		Lieut G.H. COHEN & 2/Lieut G.R. MELLOR. The advance was gallantly made but it was almost immediately annihilated by the enemy rifle & M.G. fire, and most of the men were shot down. Only a very few were able to get-more than half way across the space (about 250 yards) intervening between our line & that of the Germans. Lieut- Cohen was hit twice & killed & Capt. Brown was severely wounded. Some survivors made their way back during the day & many others after darkness had set-in. Major S.S.S. COHEN & Capt: R.S. FAIRCLOUGH, Nº656 Sergt: E. Coxon, 4931 Pte G.P. Barlow & 2778 Pte B.A. Hay made gallant-attempts to bring in wounded during broad daylight- & a few were got-in, but- the first three mentioned were wounded. We were heavily shelled by the enemy during the day from midday & between 3 P.M. & 3.30 P.M. this became intense & seemed to be the prelude to a counter attack at-dusk. This was expected, & the Bn. was in readiness.	E.R.B.
	17th May		From an early hour our guns opened a heavy fire on the enemy & the shelling was magnificent. The enemy artillery replied, & in again came under a heavy fire. About 7 A.M. the enemy hoisted numerous white flags along their trenches, & hostile of the enemy were observed running in toward the rear of their position occupied by the 7th & 8th. Many continued from part of the German line, on which also bits captured a bit of the enemy artillery & we could see a body of the 13th Kings, who had our own of the enemy line during the night, advancing along the enemy trench but-left-to-night- & more bombing was observed. The enemy trenches were heavily damaged by our gun fire - great gaps in their	

WAR DIARY or INTELLIGENCE SUMMARY

Page 2 of 17th May.

Place	Date	Hour	Summary of Events and Information	Remarks and references to Appendices
Richebourg	17th May		in their parapet being observed. We opened M.G. & rifle fire on the enemy in acc[ordance] with orders leaving a Lieutenan[t] & of the white flag of any shortly after a large number of Germans came out of their trenches towards our lines. Firing was stopped & 126 came in & surrendered. They were very much shaken, but appeared well fed & clothed. During the forenoon the Bn. advanced & occupied the captured German trench, which, both inside & out, was found to be a veritable shambles. Dead, wounded & dying were lying thick on the ground & this shows plainly the high shooting quali[ties] of our artillery. Capt. D Co. moved on to the German 2nd line trenches in support of 2/8 Staff. who had gone forward in the attack. The attack being held up by a m.g. Strong point on the enemy's new line at FERME DU BOIS, B.G. & C. retired to the pt. his German trenches leaving C.C. on the right of the 2/8 Staff. Capt. H.K.S. Woodhouse of 2/Lieut. A.H. Plummer being with the latter half of C.C. About 2 P.M. Lt. O.C. 2/8 Staff asked for a Co. to support him in return A.C. was sent out across the open. The O.C. C.S.Staff. finding A.C. & its Platoons at C.C. on his right were sufficient next A.C. Black & J. was with [?] out-L. A.C. the position it should occupy. 2/Lt. Plummer was fatally shot.[?]	Sight

Page 3. of 17th May.

WAR DIARY
or
INTELLIGENCE SUMMARY.
(Erase heading not required.)

Army Form C. 2118

Hour, Date, Place	Summary of Events and Information	Remarks and references to Appendices
Richebourg. 17th May.	The 12th the Bn. was ordered to fill up to support the 2/3 Staffs. in an attack on the Ferme du Bois, & to fill up any gap which should develop between that Bn. and the V. Inf. Bde. on the left. D Co. in the meantime to occupy the captured trench & protect its right flank of our Brigade. German bombardment.	
18th May.	Orders were received for an attack by the 4/2 Bn. & it is the former A. Co. with draw & marched back to billets at Tourret. A very heavy quantity bombardment by the enemy prevented any further relief of the Bn. Bn.s on Co. occupied the trenches all day & were subjected to a terrific bombardment. Towards dusk, after the advance from on right-hand by the 7th Division against Com d' Aronce, the 4/2 had formed up on our left at St. P.n. the Bn. (less A. Co.) commenced to withdraw, & proceeded to billets at Le Tourret.	G.R.B.
	4/2 Plummer (killed in action) did specially good work: in addition to ably discharging his duties as Platoon commander, he showed great zeal & ability in attending to the wounded. Being a medical student, his knowledge of medicine was of the utmost value. The ability bearers did their heavy work in excellent spirits. Throughout the whole time, & our Medical officer Capt. I.H. Donnell himself came up into the firing line.	

Page 2 of 18th May.

Place	Date	Hour	Summary of Events and Information	Remarks and references to Appendices
Richebourg	18 May		The behaviour of all ranks in fact was all that could be desired & great steadiness under very heavy fire was shown. Our casualties during the fighting were heavy unfortunately & were as follows :— Lieut- G. H. Cohen and 2/Lieut- A. R. Plummer. Officers killed 2 Major S. S. G. Cohen Capt. W. E. Brieg. 2/Lieut. G. F. Richardson Capt. R. F. Fairclough " D. R. Swindley. " C. A. Taylor Capt. J. H. Swindley. " W. L. Evans " C. B. Cox Capt. A. Buckley. Lieut- W Loughton. Officers wounded 11 Other Ranks. Killed. Missing, believed killed. Wounded. 41. 21. 265.	SBR CSC

WAR DIARY or INTELLIGENCE SUMMARY

Army Form C. 2118.

Page 3 of 18 May /15

Place	Date	Hour	Summary of Events and Information	Remarks and references to Appendices
RICHEBOURG			The following were recommended by the Comdg. Officer, Colonel Y. M. Mc Master V.D., for honors:—	
			Capt. W.L. EVANS — on morning of 16th May for very gallantly leading his Platoon of his Co. across the open in an assault on a section of the German trenches, and encouraging his men under very heavy rifle and machine gun fire; until he fell twice wounded. He yet remained to the German trenches. In either than any other Officer or man in that assault.	575
			2/Lieut. A.H PLUMMER — in the fighting on May 16th & 17th very gallantly attending to wounded under the fire, as well as ably carrying out his duties as Platoon commander until fatally shot on evening of 17th May.	625
			No 656 Sergt. E. COONEY) Recommended for D.C.M. for very gallant & daring out from 1452 Rfn G.P. BENSON) our trenches in broad daylight, in full view of the enemy 2778 Rfn B.A.HODS.) bringing in four of our wounded men.	

1577 Wt. W10791/1773 500,000 1/15 D. D. & L. A.D.S.S./Forms/C. 2118.

Army Form C. 2118.

WAR DIARY
or
INTELLIGENCE SUMMARY

(Erase heading not required.)

Instructions regarding War Diaries and Intelligence Summaries are contained in F. S. Regs., Part II. and the Staff Manual respectively. Title pages will be prepared in manuscript.

Hour, Date, Place		Summary of Events and Information	Remarks and references to Appendices
	1915		
LE TOURET.	19 May	The Battalion left Le Touret for new billets at Vendin-lez-Bethune	G.R.B.
VENDIN.	20 May	The Battalion left Vendin for new billets at Lozinghem.	G.R.B.
LOZINGHEM.	21 May	A general clean up and rest.	G.R.B.
"	22 May	Maj. General H.S. Horne C.B. Comdg. II Division visited the Battalion and spoke highly of the part taken by us in the fighting during 15th & 16th May. Divine Service.	G.R.B.
"	23 May		G.R.B.
"	24 May	Company training having been carried out. Fatigue parade for all Men Quarter at the Auchel Mine Baths.	G.R.B.

1247 W 3299 200,000 (E) 8/14 J.B.C. & A; Forms/C. 2118/11.

WAR DIARY
or
INTELLIGENCE SUMMARY.

Army Form C. 2118.

Place	Date May/15	Hour	Summary of Events and Information	Remarks and references to Appendices
LOZINGHEM	25		A bomb throwing demonstration was given to selected Officers of the II Inf. Bde. Afterwards Officers of the Battn. were instructed in bombing by O/C; Company training was carried out.	Q.R.3.
"	26		Coy. Officers went with the Brigade Staff to reconnoitre the French position at Sec Berlin and vicinity. Company training was carried out. In the evening Bn. Sports took place. There was very successful and much enjoyed by all ranks.	A.R.3.
"	27		Orders were received to proceed to occupy the Sussex trenches south of Vermelles — but this was almost immediately cancelled. Company training was carried out.	A.R.3.
"	28		Company training was carried out.	A.R.3.
"	29		Company training was carried out.	Q.R.3.
"	30		Received orders that the II Inf. Bde. would move to take over the Sussex trenches near Sec Berlin and Annequin and the Bn. proceeded by march route, leaving Lozinghem at 8.50 p.m. Before moving off the Brigadier came to see us and say "Good bye".	S/Apps.

1577 Wt. W10791/2773 500,000 1/15 D. D. & L. I.A.D.S.S./Forms/C. 2118.

WAR DIARY or INTELLIGENCE SUMMARY

Page 2. 30th May. Army Form C. 2118.

Place	Date	Hour	Summary of Events and Information	Remarks and references to Appendices
	30th May		He was just off to take command of the Midland Division, though in hearty congratulated him on his promotion he was nevertheless very sorry to lose him. We had listened under the heavy rain on arrival in France at the front. After a march of about 17½ miles the Battalion marched to Berlin, and at noon proceeded to the section of the trench line allotted to us at Maroc. Here we were met by guides from the French Regiment in occupation viz the 57th Regt. and on duty relieved them about midnight.	cxb
Maroc.	31st		The 57th Regt. marched off about 1 a.m. but the Grand Artillery removal in the British had not come up and was not clear to arrive for several days. The French trenches and dug-outs were beautifully made Revetting the same of safety with efficiency but - the sanitary condition left much to be desired. Our trenches were some 800 yards from the Germans and the ground had little in the way of except for a very little shelling it was been extremely quiet part of the line.	{ss}

Page 2. 31st May.

WAR DIARY
or
INTELLIGENCE SUMMARY.
(Erase heading not required.)

Army Form C. 2118.

Hour	Summary of Events and Information	Remarks and references to Appendices
	But we interrogated & found that there was a good deal of shelling. Possibly the arrival of the VI Bnd. Bde. may have been accounted for this as we do not allow the Germans opportunity in to him in peace and security if we can possibly help it.	C.S.S.

NOTES ON HOLDING "W" SECTION.

Secret.

G.S.49.

Notes on holding "W" Section.

1. There will be three subsections W.1. W.2. W.3. each held by one battalion – Berks or Rifles W.1. Staffs or 1/Kings W.2. 5th or 7th Liverpools W.3.

2. To ensure that the Brigade is at all times ready to march no platoon or machine gun detachment will be on duty in the front line of trenches for more than 24 hours at the time.
   Reliefs of Companies and Battalions will be arranged accordingly.

3. To enable the Brigade to assume the offensive at the shortest notice either in the form of a counter-attack immediately after the repulse of an enemy's attack, or to attack after two hours notice by day or night each subsection will: –

   (a) Begin at once and continue to reconnoitre to determine its objective in the enemy's lines opposite the battalion and the best way to it by day or night.

   (b) Settle and prepare all arrangements for forming up the whole battalion to issue from its front line to attack the objective selected and for holding its own line whilst the attack is carried out.

   (c) Arrange how it will get out of our own trenches and through our own wire by day or night.

   (d) Arrange the best way of supporting the other subsections and the Brigades on our right or left by fire or by moving its local reserves to support them in counter attack.

4. In case of attack: –

   (a) The front line will be held.

   (b) Should the enemy succeed in penetrating any where the subsection commanders will at once counter attack the troops in the front line use any by bombing down the trenches and by fire from their front to stop the enemy reinforcing. Subsection commanders on right and left will assist as in paragraph 3 (d) taking steps of such on the ___ of the subsection commander attacked have not been able to inform them.

   (c) The artillery will open fire in accordance with the prearranged scheme governing the subsection commander giving

(2)

giving orders direct to the R.A. Officer with him and also informing Brigade Head Quarters.

(d) The whole Brigade will get in rear of the Battalions in Reserve sending an Officer with two cyclist orderlies at once to Brigade Head Quarters.

Regulations re Stores in my recent Mem. for review Caches, helps, equipment are put from billets.

5. In the event of the enemy using gas an "G" will be sounded at stated intervals on the bugle as a signal for men to put on their masks.

Sentries will be kept on duty in the front trench and other available places who will sound the order of the Officer on duty in the front trench & will on hearing the call or hearing it —

Men will at once put on their masks and the companies get ready for action.

6. The proposed amendments to Para 3 in paragraph 3 will be reported to the G.O.C. as soon as possible after receipt & will be given opportunity them before being put into action.

24/7/15.
Brigade Major
Brigade Major 1st Inf. Bde.

6th Infantry Brigade.
2nd Division.

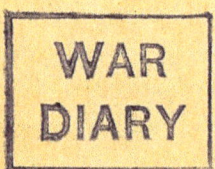

5th BATTN. THE KING'S (LIVERPOOL REGIMENT).

J U N E

1 9 1 5

5th Battn. The King's (Liverpool Regiment).

June 1915

Place	Date			Summary
Nouex	June	1		General Horne, General Lord Cavan, and lately IV General Brigadier, and our new Brigadier, General Daly, came round our position. C.S.G.
"		2		Trench duty continued. C.S.G.
"		3		Trench duty continued. C.S.G.
"		4		After dark we were relieved by the 7th & hant R. and marched back to billets at Les Brebis. C.S.G.
Les Brebis		5		The Bn. had a general clean up, and then started on Company training. Major Blunt 2nd in Command was appointed by the Brigadier, special

Page. 2. 5 June.

WAR DIARY or INTELLIGENCE SUMMARY
Army Form C. 2118.

Place	Date	Hour	Summary of Events and Information	Remarks and references to Appendices
Maroc.			Intelligence Officer. Col: Fox Mackers & Capt: Brenan, Adjt, went to reconnoitre a new line of trenches in the vicinity of Vermelles held by the 147 Brigade. 2/Lieuts Butterly and Rowe joined the Battalion from England and brought a party of 31 other ranks who had left in a rush or wounded. At 9 p.m. received orders that the Brigade would be relieved about 11 p.m. on 6th inst. and would then march to Lillers from Noeux les Mines.	a.a.o.
Maroc.	June 6.		Company training was carried out. At 11 p.m. the Bn. was relieved by the 18th London Reg.t and at 11.15 p.m. we marched off to Noeux les Mines.	G.S.63
Noeux les Mines.	7.		Arrived at Lillers about 4.45 a.m. At 10.30 a.m. we were notified by the Brigade that the Bn would on July K.6.1. on Hon. Colonel was coming to us and that himself and another about 2 p.m. The Battalion was drawn up in	a.a.m.s. S/C R

Page 2 June 7th.

Army Form C. 2118.

WAR DIARY
or
INTELLIGENCE SUMMARY.
(Erase heading not required.)

Place	Date	Hour	Summary of Events and Information	Remarks and references to Appendices
Noeux les Mines			Rollcalls gone over. No time wasted. Lord Derby first inspected the Battalion and then told us how pleased he was to be our Hon. Colonel, especially so after its fine work done by the 5th during the war. He informed us that the General had spoken highly of our conduct & had said he was well satisfied with us. After leaving he shook hands with all the Officers. General Munro, General Horne, General Daly, and a number of Staff were present. After Lord Derby had left General Munro remained behind & spoke for some time to Colonel McMaster.	G.S.O.3
	June 8		Company training was carried out. Orders received that we were to move to Vermelles. At 9 p.m. the Battalion moved off and arrived at Vermelles at midnight.	9.S.O.3
	9.		Spent the day cleaning up billets and the ground surrounding same. Everything was most quiet.	G.S.O.3
	10.		Company training was carried out, also numerous fatigues were found for the R.E.	G.S.O.3

1577 Wt. W10791/1773 500,000 1/15 D. D. & L. A.D.S.S./Forms/C. 2118.

Army Form C. 2118.

WAR DIARY
or
INTELLIGENCE SUMMARY.
(Erase heading not required.)

Instructions regarding War Diaries and Intelligence Summaries are contained in F. S. Regs., Part II. and the Staff Manual respectively. Title pages will be prepared in manuscript.

Place	Date	Hour	Summary of Events and Information	Remarks and references to Appendices
VERMELLES	June/15		Relieved the 2/S. Staffs, taking over their duty in the trenches. Enemy was particularly quiet.	G.S.B.
"	12		On duty in the trenches. The Sergt Major and three other ranks wounded. Casualties.	G.S.B.
"	13		On duty in the trenches. Very quiet. Lieut. Vermelles was shelled. Casualties. One man wounded.	G.S.B.
"	14		On duty in the trenches. Received orders to the effect that VI Inf. Brigade (ours) would be relieved by the V.I. Brunos on night. 2nd Worcestershire Regt. to proceed to billets at Sanqueneuil. Enemy particularly quiet.	G.S.B.
"	15	At 9.20 p.m. the head of 2/Worc. R. arrived at Vermelles & was led by our guides and ld- to the trenches. By 11.15 pm the relief was completed and Coy on marching off individually, marched Tauquereuil between 4.30 A.M. and 5.30 A.M. on 16. inst.	5/8/2 G.S.B.

1577 Wt.W10791/1773 500,000 1/15 D. D. & L. A.D.S.S./Forms/C. 2118.

Army Form C. 2118.

WAR DIARY
or
INTELLIGENCE SUMMARY.
(Erase heading not required.)

Instructions regarding War Diaries and Intelligence Summaries are contained in F. S. Regs., Part II. and the Staff Manual respectively. Title pages will be prepared in manuscript.

Place	Date June/15	Hour	Summary of Events and Information	Remarks and references to Appendices
FAUQUEREUIL	16.		Rested and cleaned up.	
"			The inhabitants here do not welcome us very cordially. They complain that they have had troops billeted on them ever since the war started whereas neighbouring villages have not, it they say it is the turn of the latter.	C.C.B.
"	17.		Company training.	
"	18.		Company training.	
"	19.		Left during the morning for Annequin — less the 2. M. Dep^{ts} & transport kⁱ	
ANNEQUIN			Vermelles.	
"			Furnished working party for R.E.	C.C.B.
"	20.		Divine Service.	
"			R.E. working party found.	C.C.B.
"	21.		Company training.	
"			Found R.E. working parties.	
"	22		Relieved the 7th & 1st Q. in Cuinchy trenches — march and south of the	C.C.B.
CUINCHY			LA BASSEE — BETHUNE road.	
			2/L^{ts} Walker, McIntosh and Hudson reported for duty from the 2/5 L. and R.	C.C.B.

Army Form C. 2118.

WAR DIARY
or
INTELLIGENCE SUMMARY.
(Erase heading not required.)

Place	Date	Hour	Summary of Events and Information	Remarks and references to Appendices
CUINCHY	23.		Duty in trenches.	G.S.B.
"	24		Duty in trenches.	G.S.B.
"	25		Casualties - Other ranks, three wounded. Duty in trenches.	
"			Casualties - Other ranks, three wounded.	G.S.B.
"	26		2nd Lts. Duffin and Transport proceeded from Vergignuil to Bevrry. The Bn. on relief by 7th Bn. R. Inniskilling Killies at Anne gun posts at night when came in that. Bn. went to take over to Supporting Area - Annequin. Cambrin Tourbieres - on 27 inst from 1. R. Berks.	G.S.B.
TOURBIERES and vicinity	27.		Took over Support Area from 1. R. Berks. Bn. Hq. Rue dt Tourbieres A C. } B. C. } dt Cambrin dt Cuinchy Support Point C. C. dt Cambrin Support Point D. C. dt Tourbieres.	G.S.B.
"	28		The Bn. found Mining Fatigue Parties for R.E. Fatigue parties found for R.E. The Enemy sprung a mine injuring four of our men.	G.S.B.
"	29		One man No 2496 Rfn. Harris died of his wound - the result of an accident in rifle grenade firing last for 2 Lt. Gunn.	G.S.B. G.S.B.

Army Form C. 2118.

WAR DIARY
or
INTELLIGENCE SUMMARY.
(Erase heading not required.)

Instructions regarding War Diaries and Intelligence Summaries are contained in F. S. Regs., Part II. and the Staff Manual respectively. Title pages will be prepared in manuscript.

Place	Date	Hour	Summary of Events and Information	Remarks: references Appendix
CUINCHY	June/15 30.		Relieved 7th & 8th hon Regt in the Cuinchy Trenches	G.S.B.

6th Infantry Brigade.
2nd Division.

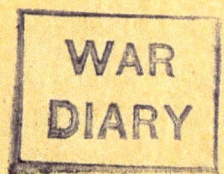

5th BATTN. THE KING'S (LIVERPOOL REGIMENT).

JULY

1915

5th Battn. The King's (Liverpool Regiment).

July 1915

CUINCHY.	July 1st	Bn. in trench duty. Casualties - 3 other ranks wounded	R.S.B.
"	2	Bn. on trench duty.	A.S.B.
"	3	Bn. on trench duty. Casualties - Other ranks, wounded two.	A.S.B.
"	.	The enemy heavily shelled our during day, it lay night offered a heavy MG rifle & grenade fire. to which we replied.	A.S.B.
"	4	Bn. on trench duty. Casualties - Other ranks, wounded two.	A.S.B.
"	5	Bn. relieved in trenches. VI Sgt. Bde on relief by 4th Guards Brigade. 5 coys march to rest at Bethune.	A.S.B.
BETHUNE	6	General rest and clean up. A proportion of men going to baths at Lot. Field Ambulance on at Ecole de jeunes filles.	6/7/15 A.S.B.
"	7	XX bns the and more of new clothing. Remainder of Bn. bathed at No 4 Field Ambulance and Ecole de jeunes Filles	A.S.B.

Army Form C. 2118.

WAR DIARY
or
INTELLIGENCE SUMMARY.
(Erase heading not required.)

Instructions regarding War Diaries and Intelligence Summaries are contained in F.S. Regs., Part II. and the Staff Manual respectively. Title pages will be prepared in manuscript.

Place	Date	Hour	Summary of Events and Information	Remarks and references to Appendices
BÉTHUNE	July/15 8.	10.30 A.m.	Bn. paraded at Barracks to march off for inspection by Lord Kitchener. The inspection took place about 12.15 P.M. after which Bn. returned to Barracks.	G.S.13.
"		9	Company training and route marches. Bomb throwing lectures.	G.S.13.
"		10	Company training carried out. Attended by visit to Swimming Baths & to Welsh Fete. Bn Bn. vs. 1st K Liverp.	G.S.13.
"		11	Church Parade.	G.S.13.
"		12	Route lectures and practice with dummy bombs.	G.S.13.
"			Route march. In the afternoon VI Inf. Bde. Brigade Sports.	G.S.13. 5/8th
"		13	VI Inf. Bde. relieves V Inf. Bde. 3 P.M. Bn. moves to Le Preol, taking over billets there from the 9 Winchesters.	G.S.13.
		10.30 P.m.	ordered to send up 2 Platoons to garrison Orchard Farm Redoubt on 7th & 8th R to march to hold line. Sent 3 Platoons D. Co. about 167 in all.	G.S.13.

Army Form C. 2118.

WAR DIARY
or
INTELLIGENCE SUMMARY.
(Erase heading not required.)

Instructions regarding War Diaries and Intelligence Summaries are contained in F. S. Regs., Part II. and the Staff Manual respectively. Title pages will be prepared in manuscript.

Place	Date	Hour	Summary of Events and Information	Remarks and references to Appendices
LE PRÉOL	July/15 14.		Moved up remainder of D. Co. to Orchard Farm Redoubt to carry on mining work southwards and forward to. Found very heavy mining fatigues under R.E. which necessitated using up every available man including Stretcher Bearers and some of the Officers servants.	A.S.B.
"	15		Mining fatigues.	A.S.B.
"	16		Mining fatigues. Casualties — Other ranks, one wounded.	A.S.B.
	17		Relieved 7th to hand in Givenchy trenches. Casualties — Other ranks, one killed — No 595-8/Cpl. Reynolds by shell fire.	A.S.B.
GUINCHY	18		Bn. on trench duty.	A.S.B. 5/8/15
"	19		Bn. on trench duty.	C.S.B.
"	20		Bn. on trench duty. Casualties — Other ranks, one wounded.	A.S.B.

Army Form C. 2118.

WAR DIARY
or
INTELLIGENCE SUMMARY.
(Erase heading not required.)

Instructions regarding War Diaries and Intelligence Summaries are contained in F. S. Regs., Part II. and the Staff Manual respectively. Title pages will be prepared in manuscript.

Place	Date	Hour	Summary of Events and Information	Remarks and references to Appendices
GUINCHY	July/15	21	On relief by 7/9. D. bat. R. 2 Platoons of A Co. are left to garrison ORCHARD REDOUBT. Remainder of A Co. and D Co. proceed to billets at LE PREOL under command of Major J.T. SHUTE. The Machine Gun Section goes to LE PREOL whilst Bn. H.Q., Bn. and B. and C. Co. are billeted in part of the College de Jeunes Filles. BETHUNE — An other part of the building being occupied by the 2nd Worcestershire. 2/Lieuts STARKES and BOND join the Bn:	E.S.B.
BETHUNE & LE PREOL		22	Bn rests & cleans up generally. About 5.30 P.M. the Germans shell the College de Jeunes Filles and vicinity. One shell hitting the top of the building occupied by the 2nd Worcestershire and one falling into the grounds on the Worcestershire side. Unfortunately kill 8 men killed outright and some 50 wounded of whom some died during the night. Our casualties were only one man very slightly wounded. At 6.40 P.M received orders from 2/ Division direct to move off as soon as possible to LE PREOL. At 8.40 P.M. marched off	5/3/12 E.S.B.

Army Form C. 2118.

WAR DIARY
or
INTELLIGENCE SUMMARY.
(Erase heading not required.)

Instructions regarding War Diaries and Intelligence Summaries are contained in F. S. Regs., Part II. and the Staff Manual respectively. Title pages will be prepared in manuscript.

Place	Date	Hour	Summary of Events and Information	Remarks and references to Appendices
LE PREOL	July/15 23.		Company training and Inspection carried out.	A.S.B.
"	24		Company training carried out. Aquatic sports in the afternoon. Inter Keep and Meade Aimed in Bn.	A.S.B.
"	25		Relieved 7/L'pool R. in Cunninghy trenches. Sec. B. 1 relieving from La Bassee Canal to Finchley Road trench.	A.S.B.
GUINCHY	26		Bn. on trench duty. Casualties — one man wounded.	A.S.B.
	27.		Bn. on trench duty. General Gough made an inspection of the line of trenches. During the evening the enemy sprung a mine to our left, by King's Road R. Casualties — two other ranks wounded.	S.B.R
	28.		Bn. on trench duty. Enemy artillery fire on heavy during the evening, and to our left	A.S.B.

Army Form C. 2118.

WAR DIARY
or
INTELLIGENCE SUMMARY.
(Erase heading not required.)

O & a July-continued.

Instructions regarding War Diaries and Intelligence Summaries are contained in F. S. Regs., Part II. and the Staff Manual respectively. Title pages will be prepared in manuscript.

Place	Date	Hour	Summary of Events and Information	Remarks and references to Appendices
	July/15		exploded another mine some 20 yards short of the trench occupied by 1/K.R.R. The K.R.R. at once occupied the crater formed by this mine.	
CUIVENCHY	29th		The enemy heavily shelled our line, and behind our line during the early morning. Bn. relieved by "Cameron" Highlanders & Cameron & Glasgow Highlanders at 12.30 p.m. The VI Sgt. Bde on relief by 4th Guards Brigade & Glasgow Highlanders from V Sgt. Bde went back for a rest. We went to VENDIN when in turn we billets from the 3rd Coldstream Guards. Colonel Franklin proceeding on leave, Major Shute took over command of the Bn. Casualties – Other ranks, one wounded.	G.S.C.B. 5/8/15

1577 Wt.W10791/1773 500,000 1/15 D. D. & L. A.D.S.S./Forms/C. 2118.

Army Form C. 2118.

WAR DIARY
or
INTELLIGENCE SUMMARY.
(Erase heading not required.)

Place	Date	Hour	Summary of Events and Information	Remarks and references to Appendices
VENDIN.	July/15 30.		The Bn. bathed, rested and cleaned up generally.	A.A.8
	31.		Adjutants Class for Subaltern Officers & selective N.C.O.s Company training. Kit Inspections. Dusing in afternoon rested.	G.S.B.

6th Infantry Brigade.
2nd Division.

WAR DIARY

5th BATTN. THE KING'S (LIVERPOOL REGIMENT).

A U G U S T

1 9 1 5

Attached:
Appendices 4, 5, 6 & 7.

Army Form C. 2118.

WAR DIARY
or
INTELLIGENCE SUMMARY.
(Erase heading not required.)

Instructions regarding War Diaries and Intelligence Summaries are contained in F. S. Regs., Part II. and the Staff Manual respectively. Title pages will be prepared in manuscript.

Place	Date	Hour	Summary of Events and Information	Remarks and references to Appendices
VENDIN	August 1915 1.		Early morning physical exercise parades, and Adjutants class for Officers & N.C.O.s. Divine Service. In the afternoon Bn. Sports. The men, who were getting rather sick of doing nothing, have now quite got over this, and are now cheery and fit to do anything. Sgt. Nutt is doing all ranks a deal of good.	C.R.S.
	2.		Adjutants Class. Company training. Instruction in Bombing and Grenade throwing. During the former two N.C.O.s were unfortunately wounded by a bomb exploding through careless handling. Bn. rested during afternoon. Orders received that Bn. were posted to 1st Div. of BEUVRY by 12 midnight 3/4 August to commence training as a Pioneer Battalion - being transferred thither from V Corps. 4 working under C.R.E. 2/ Division. For detail orders see APPX 4	A.D.S.S./Forms/C. 2118. q.e.a. APPX 4

(J.M.)

Army Form C 2118.

WAR DIARY
or
INTELLIGENCE SUMMARY
(Erase heading not required).

Instructions regarding War Diaries and Intelligence Summaries are contained in F.S. Regs., Part II and the Staff Manual respectively. Title Pages will be prepared in manuscript.

Place.	Date 1915	Hour	Summary of Events and Information.	Remarks and references to Appendices
VENDIN.	Aug. 3.		Adjutants Class & Lectures & selected N.C.O's. Company training. The VI Infantry Brigade held a horse show at the Sports Ground BETHUNE. In the afternoon all ranks were allowed to attend. A very excellent programme was carried. The 1/R Berks were At Home and the band of the 1/Kings played a the above engagement. The Battalion carried off two first prizes and two second. The Bn. paraded at 6.30 P.M. and marched off to BEUVRY at 6.45 P.M. arriving at 8 P.M. in heavy rain — less the M.G. Sec which remained behind at VENDIN and was attached to 1/K.R.R.	G.S.S
			Casualties — Other ranks — Review risk.	
BEUVRY.	4.		Commenced Pioneer work. A and B Companies working after PONT FIXE and HARLEY STREET CUINCHY defenses under the East Anglian Co. Royal Engineers, and C and D Companies working	

(Initial)

WAR DIARY
or
INTELLIGENCE SUMMARY
Army Form C 2118.

Place	Date	Hour	Summary of Events and Information	Remarks and references to Appendices
	Aug/15		Line between BRADELL POINT, HARLEY STREET and CUINCHY SUPPORT POINT manned by 118 Field Co. R.E. Training of Signallers was carried out. During the afternoon Sgt Y and Lt Brigade Major came to inspect. One man to hospital - accidentally kicked by a horse. He was cleaning.	Appx 3.
BEUVRY	5		Company work and disposition having carried on. Pioneer Coy to Officers under Lt Sylvester Lt DARLINGTON R.E. 2/3 Division and details at GORRE. All our senior officers who could be spared were ordered to attend. Casualties - Officer nil, other ranks - Died - one.	Appx 3.

J.M.M.

Army Form C 2118.

WAR DIARY
or
INTELLIGENCE SUMMARY
(Erase heading not required).

Instructions regarding War Diaries and Intelligence Summaries are contained in F.S. Regs., Part II and the Staff Manual respectively. Title Pages will be prepared in manuscript.

Place.	Date.	Hour.	Summary of Events and Information.	Remarks and references to Appendices
BÉSVAS.	Aug 9/15	Continued	A Draft of 20 - consisting of S.M. Kelly, 20 of our men who had been transferred to England returned and transferred to England with permits to Battn. from the 3/5 & from R. from WEETON.	e.s.B.
		5.	Officers Pioneer Class continued. Work continued on CUINCHY defences. Signallers training carried out. Augmented Signal drill carried out in the evening. Carnoustie - Other Ranks - Bombers - Snipers.	e.s.B
		7.	Officers Pioneer Class continued. Work continued on CUINCHY defences. Augmented Signal drill continued in evening. The Machine Gun Section proceeded to duty in CUINCHY trenches. its Reserve being billeted at ANNEQUIN. The Section is now under the dis- orders of the VI Bgd. Bde. Machine Gun Officer.	e.s.B.

WAR DIARY
or
INTELLIGENCE SUMMARY
(Erase heading not required).

Army Form C 2118.

Place.	Date	Hour	Summary of Events and Information.	Remarks and references to Appendices
BEUVRY.	Aug 7.		Physical training was carried out before breakfast. Divine Service took place. Company training carried out from 9 am to 10.15 am.	Q.S.G.
	9.		Colonel McMASTER returned from leave to ENGLAND and resumed command of the Battn. to his absence Major SHUTE commanded the Battn. M. Pioneer Class continued. General HORNE, G.O.C. H Division inspected Gas Class at work. Rgt'l Class of N.C.Os. in the evening. Work on CUINCHY Defences continued. Signalling training continued. Casualties — Other Ranks — 3 our ranks. a Draft of 81 joined the Battn. — 79 from 2/5 Bn & 1 at had R.'. from the 2 base, ROUEN (one unsuitable and one sick) CANTERBURY.	S.S.G.

9 m m

Army Form C 2118.

WAR DIARY
or
INTELLIGENCE SUMMARY
(Erase heading not required).

Instructions regarding War Diaries and Intelligence Summaries are contained in F.S. Regs., Part II and the Staff Manual respectively. Title Pages will be prepared in manuscript.

Place.	Date	Hour	Summary of Events and Information.	Remarks and references to Appendices
BEUVRY	Aug. 10		Officer Pioneer Class continued. Work on CUINCHY Defences continued. Signalling training carried out. Rifle Class of Instruction for N.C.O.s. Advanced Squad Drill. Casualties - Other Ranks - Two sick.	App.63.
"	11		Officer Pioneer Class continued. Work on CUINCHY Defences continued. Signalling training carried out. Rifle Class of Instruction for N.C.O.s. Advanced Squad Drill. Casualties - Other ranks - One sick.	App.63.

WAR DIARY
or
INTELLIGENCE SUMMARY
(Erase heading not required).

Army Form C 2118

Place.	Date Aug 6	Hour	Summary of Events and Information.	Remarks and references to Appendices
BEUVRY.	12.		Officers Classes and Work on CUINCHY Defences continued. Signalling training carried out. Regular Class of Instruction for N.C.Os. Awkward Squad drill. Orders received that from to-morrow 17. Bn. would be lent to VI Infy. Bde. to relieve 1st 1/K.R.R. The C.O. and Adjt. inspected work done by Cos. and called at N.d. Qrs. 1/K.R.R. at WOBURN ABBEY before relieving them. Casualties — Other Ranks — four sick.	G.S.B.
BEUVRY & CUINCHY	13		Bn. H.d. Qrs. and A and B Cos. relieved 1/K.R.R. H.d. Qrs. and 2 Cos. in Section A.1. CUINCHY. 1/K.R.R. left one Co. at CAMBRIN and one at TOURBIÈRES under command of Colonel McMASTER. C. & D. Cos. continued work on CUINCHY DEFENCES. Officers River Class continued. Casualties — Other Ranks — Sick, one.	G.S.B.
	14		Trench duty and work on CUINCHY Defences continued. Officers River Class continued.	G.S.B.

Army Form C 2118.

WAR DIARY
or
INTELLIGENCE SUMMARY
(Erase heading not required).

Instructions regarding War Diaries and Intelligence Summaries are contained in F.S. Regs., Part II and the Staff Manual respectively. Title Pages will be prepared in manuscript.

Place.	Date Aug 1915	Hour	Summary of Events and Information.	Remarks and references to Appendices
CUINCHY & BEUVRY	15.		C and D Coys relieved A & B - then left his named proceeding to BEUVRY. Trench duty & work on CUINCHY defences continued. Officers & Pioneer Class continued. Casualties - Other Ranks - Sick. 3.	C.S.B.
"	16.		Trench duty & work on CUINCHY defences continued. Officers Pioneer Class continued. Casualties - Other Ranks - Wounded & at duty. One. Sick. One.	C.S.B.
"	17.		Bn. Hd. Qrs. and C and D Coys were relieved by 1/ K.R.R. and proceeded to billets at BEUVRY. Work on CUINCHY defences continued. Casualties - Other Ranks - Sick. 2. In afternoon C and D Coys went into BETHUNE for baths.	C.S.B.
BEUVRY.	18		Work on CUINCHY defences continued. Signalling training carried out. 4th Guards Brigade on leaving the II Division to morrow morning. VI Sig. Bde sent telegram wishing them good luck. 4th Guards Bde. reply All Bns. of the Brigade had orders to send 1 Officer & 20 men into BETHUNE to night.	APPX:506.

J.A.M.

Army Form C 2118.

WAR DIARY
or
INTELLIGENCE SUMMARY
(Erase heading not required).

Instructions regarding War Diaries and Intelligence Summaries are contained in F.S. Regs., Part II and the Staff Manual respectively. Title Pages will be prepared in manuscript.

Place.	Date	Hour	Summary of Events and Information.	Remarks and references to Appendices
BEUVRY	Aug. 18.	Continued.	who are to join the Guards a "send-off" lr. morrow morning. Lt. KEET and 20 N.C.Os & men were sent by the Canadians - Other Ranks - Killed. No 2764 Pte COPELAND which on far in BETHUNE was killed by a bomb dropped from an enemy aeroplane. Wounded - One Sick - Two.	e.s.B.
"	19.		Work carried on at CUINCHY defences. Signalling training carried out. Bayld Class of Instruction of N.C.Os. Awakened Squad Drill. Army received the Lord KITCHENER would be passing through the area but at the last moment this was changed. Army received that Bn. is now directly under the II Division for administration purposes.	APPX. 7. e.s.B.
"	20.		Work continued on CUINCHY defences Signalling training carried out. Rifle Class of Instruction of N.C.Os. Awakened Squad Drill. Casualties - Other Ranks - Sick - 2.	e.s.B.

WAR DIARY
or
INTELLIGENCE SUMMARY
(Erase heading not required).

Army Form C 2118.

Place.	Date Aug 1915	Hour	Summary of Events and Information.	Remarks and references to Appendices
BEUVRY	21.		Work continued on CUINCHY defences. Signalling training carried out. Rapid fire of Instruction for N.C.Os. Casualties – Other Ranks – Sick 4.	Authorised Squad Drill. e.s.B.
"	22.		Physical exercise before breakfast. Divine Service. Our C.o.E. Church. the C.O. Col. McMASTER. handed the D.C.M. to Cpl. McGUIRE which he gained for very gallant conduct in getting in a wounded man in full view of the enemy, & very clear range, & in broad daylight, at CUINCHY on March 23rd/15. Company training carried out. A.G. continued work on CUINCHY defences. Casualties – Other Ranks – Sick – One –	e.s.B.
"	23.		Work continued on CUINCHY defences. Signalling training carried out. Rapid fire of Instruction for N.C.Os.	Authorised Squad Drill. e.s.B.

WAR DIARY
or
INTELLIGENCE SUMMARY
(Erase heading not required).

Army Form C 2118.

Instructions regarding War Diaries and Intelligence Summaries are contained in F.S. Regs., Part II and the Staff Manual respectively. Title Pages will be prepared in manuscript.

Place.	Date	Hour	Summary of Events and Information.	Remarks and references to Appendices
BEUVRY	Aug 24th		Work on CUINCHY Defences continued. Signalling training carried out. Regtl. Class of Instruction of N.C.Os. The Machine Gun Section of its draft 90 unit Wants to BETHUNE on instructional Squad drill being retired by XIX Inf. Bde. Casualties - Sick. Other Ranks - Two.	A.T.B.
"	25th		Work continued on CUINCHY Defences. Signalling training carried out. M.G. training carried out. Regtl. Class of Instruction for N.C.Os. Notification received from II Division that the Bn will be attached to VI Inf. Bde. temporarily for all purposes - with effect from 28th inst. Casualties - Other Ranks - Sick - 2.	
"	26th		VI Inf. Bde. op. tooks at LILLERS neighbourhood for a rest. The Bn is attached from the VI Inf. Bde. M.G. Section rejoins the Bn.	b.r.B.

9. m. m.

Army Form C 2118.

WAR DIARY
or
INTELLIGENCE SUMMARY
(Erase heading not required).

Instructions regarding War Diaries and Intelligence Summaries are contained in F.S. Regs., Part II and the Staff Manual respectively. Title Pages will be prepared in manuscript.

Place.	Date	Hour	Summary of Events and Information.	Remarks and references to Appendices
BEUVRY	Aug 26		*continued* Work continued on CUINCHY defences. Signalling training carried out. Reg'l Class of Instruction of N.C.Os. Awkward Squad Drill. Casualties — Other Ranks — Sick — One.	C.E.B.
"	27.		Work commenced on 900 x in length at CUINCHY. Signalling & M.G. training carried out. Reg'l Class of Instruction of N.C.Os. Awkward Squad Drill.	R.E.B.
"	28.		Work continued on communication trench. Signalling & M.G. training carried out. Reg'l Class of Instruction of N.C.Os. Awkward Squad Drill. Inspection of bicycles in charge by the Armourer Serg'. Casualties — Other Ranks — Sick — Two.	R.E.B.
"	29.		Divine Service. Work continued on communication trench. Casualties — Other Ranks — Sick — Two.	R.E.B.

Army Form C2118.

WAR DIARY
or
INTELLIGENCE SUMMARY
(Erase heading not required).

Instructions regarding War Diaries and Intelligence Summaries are contained in F.S. Regs., Part II and the Staff Manual respectively. Title Pages will be prepared in manuscript.

Place	Date	Hour	Summary of Events and Information.	Remarks and references to Appendices
	Aug 1915			
BEUVRY	30.		Work continued on communication trench at CUINCHY. M.G. & Signalling training carried out. Rapid aim for instruction of N.C.Os. Ankward Squad drill.	E.S.B.

APPENDICES

4
5
6
7

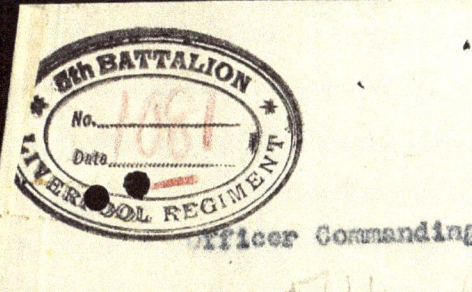 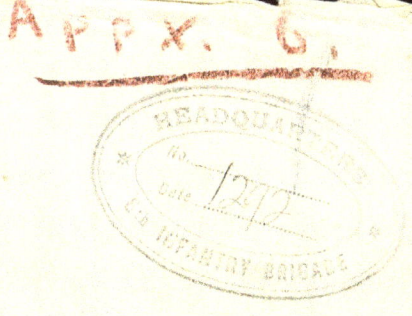

APPX. G.

Officer Commanding
5/L'pool

The following is a copy of a wire received from 4th (Guards) Brigade in reply to the farewell message sent by the Brigadier General Commanding on behalf of the 6th Infantry Brigade:-

" All ranks 4th (Guards) Brigade thank 6th Brigade for their telegram AAA We all regret very much having to leave our old comrades of the 5th and 6th Brigades with whom we have lived so long AAA We shall always watch with the greatest interest the doings of your gallant Brigade who have already done so much to make the name of the 2nd Division famous AAA Au Revoir."

H. Aui Potter, Captain,
a/Brigade Major 6th Infantry Brigade.

18.8.1915.

"A" Form.   Army Form C. 2121.

MESSAGES AND SIGNALS.

APPX 7.

TO: 5th KINGS (1st BDE)

Sender's Number	Day of Month	In reply to Number	AAA
A144	19th		

From to-day inclusive the 1/5th Kings will come directly under the Division and will no longer be attached to 1st Brigade. Men sent down to sick dressing station and from to-day the works will be attached to the RE.

"A" Form.   Army Form C. 2121.
MESSAGES AND SIGNALS,   APPX 4.   No. of Message

Prefix	Code	m.	Words.	Charge.	This message is on a/c of:	Recd. at	m.
Office of Origin and Service Instructions.			Sent			Date	
			At	m.	Service.	From	YB
			To			By	
			By		(Signature of "Franking Officer.")		

TO { CRE
5th Liverpools
7th Liverpools }

Sender's Number   Day of Month   In reply to Number   **A A A**

Instructions having been received to train the battalions in pioneer duties 5th and 7th Battalions Liverpool regiment have been selected aaa These battalions will be detached temporarily from 6th Infy Bde and will be trained in general pioneer work by employment on divisional defence work under superintendence of C.R.E. aaa 6th Bde will please arrange for 7th Liverpools to be billeted in ESSARS and CROIX de FER area and in conjunction with 5th Bde for 5th Liverpool to billet in BEUVRY before midnight 3/4th August at which hour these battalions will come direct under orders of Div HQ aaa Programme of training combined with work will be prepared and submitted

From
Place
Time
The above may be forwarded as now corrected. (Z)

Censor. Signature of Addressor or person authorised to telegraph in his name
* This line should be erased if not required.

"A" Form.   Army Form C. 2121.

MESSAGES AND SIGNALS.

Prefix	Code	m.	Words.	Charge.	This message is on a/c of:	Recd. at	m.
Office of Origin and Service Instructions.			Sent		Service.	Date	
			At ___ m.			From	
			To		(Signature of "Franking Officer.")	By	

TO { 2

| Sender's Number | Day of Month | In reply to Number | AAA |

to Div. HQ by CRE who will communicate direct with the battalions as to the daily parties required and hour and rendezvous at which each is to report aaa Addressed 4th Bde and RE repeated 4th Bde 5th Bde 5th and 7th Liverpools

From 2nd Div
Place
Time 7.30 pm

Loustauphan
Lt Col
Genl Staff

"A" Form. Army Form C.2121.
MESSAGES AND SIGNALS.
No. of Message

Prefix	Code		This message is on a/c of:	Recd. at 3.30 p.m.
Office of Origin and Service Instructions		Sent		Date 15/8/15
6th B.	No.	At m.	Service.	From Bde
	Date	To		By Taylor AD
		By	(Signature of "Franking Officer.")	

TO { ALL BATTALIONS

Sender's Number	Day of Month	In reply to Number	
A 241	15th		AAA

Following wire to 11th Brigade begins aaa All ranks 6th Brigade view your approaching departure from the division with greatest regret and we wish you good luck and Godspeed wherever you go aaa Au Revoir aaa Ends

From
Place 6th BDE
Time   3-10 p.m.

The above may be forwarded as now corrected. (Z)
Censor. Signature of Addressor or person authorised to telegraph in his name
* This line should be erased if not required.

6th Infantry Brigade.

2nd Division.

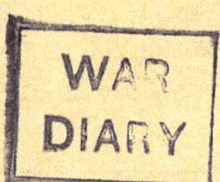

5th BATTN. THE KING'S (LIVERPOOL REGIMENT).

S E P T E M B E R

1 9 1 5

WAR DIARY
or
INTELLIGENCE SUMMARY
(Erase heading not required).

Army Form C 2118.

Instructions regarding War Diaries and Intelligence Summaries are contained in F.S. Regs., Part II and the Staff Manual respectively. Title Pages will be prepared in manuscript.

Place.	Date	Hour	Summary of Events and Information.	Remarks and references to Appendices
BEUVRY	September 1915			
	1		Work continued on communication trench at CUINCHY. M.G. & Signallers training carried out. Rifle Class of Instruction for N.C.O. C.O. & 2nd in Command inspected work done on trench. Casualties — Other Ranks — Sick — One.	G.e.B.
"	2		Work continued on communication trench at CUINCHY. M.G. & Signallers training carried out. Rifle Class of Instruction of N.C.O. The C.O. attended a Conference of Cavalry Officers at VII Inf. Bde. H.Q. Qrs. at LA LETTE. Casualties — Other Ranks — Sick — None. Authorised Squad Drill.	G.e.B.
"	3		Work continued on communication trench at CUINCHY. M.G. & Signaller training carried out. Rifle Class of Instruction to N.C.O. Scout orders regarding Operations were notified by the C.O. to Senior Major, Adj: and Coy Commdrs. Casualties — Other Ranks — Sick — One. Authorised Squad Drill.	G.e.B.

Army Form C 2118.

WAR DIARY
or
INTELLIGENCE SUMMARY
(Erase heading not required).

Instructions regarding War Diaries and Intelligence Summaries are contained in F.S. Regs., Part II and the Staff Manual respectively. Title Pages will be prepared in manuscript.

Place	Date	Hour	Summary of Events and Information.	Remarks and references to Appendices
Beuvry	Sept. 4.		Work continued on communication trench at Cuinchy. The Bn. rejoin VI Inf. Bde. M.G. Section and 2 guns for duty under Bde. M.G. Officer in support trench. 1/Ki. Rowe attached to 2/Division Signal Co. for special observation duty. 7 men from Rainfirth rejoin Bn. (one returned from England) Rgt'd. Serjt. of Instruction & N.C.O. Rainfirth signal still.	G.S.B.
"	5.		Divine Services held. Company training during morning. In afternoon Bn. employed on working parties for VI Inf. Bde.	G.S.B.
"	6th		Attack on Rainfirth site the. Bombing instruction carried out. Company training. Working parties found for Cuinchy defences. Two men to Rainfirth sick.	G.S.B.
"	7.		Company training. Bombing instruction.	G.S.B.
Cuinchy	8.		Went into the Cuinchy trenches - Sec. A.1 - taking over from 1/Kings. Transport & Q.M. staff remaining at Beuvry. Two men on mine duty were overcome by the foul air but after a rest were able to continue at duty.	G.S.B.

Stationery Services Press, X 8. 5,000 7/15

WAR DIARY or INTELLIGENCE SUMMARY

Army Form C 2118.

Place	Date Sept.	Hour	Summary of Events and Information.	Remarks and references to Appendices
Cuinchy	9		Trench duty. During last evening & night the enemy were very active with trench mortars to which in reality replied. Altogether the night was somewhat of a disturbed nature. A good deal of activity was displayed by both sides during the day. One of our trenches was blown in & one of our trench mortars was blown to pieces & buried. Casualties. One killed by trench mortar No 2591 Rfn. Johnson. One wounded – shock – at duty. One sick – to hospital.	e.s.B.
"	10		Very disturbed day. A number of our trenches being blown in. We were very lucky to have no casualties. Enemy aeroplane shot down at "Windy Corner" Givenchy. We were told the crew of German were in Galicia transferred with German permission from Bde. Hd. Qrs. to read this one to the enemy our Rfn & have obtained permission to manure out of a catapult.	e.s.B.
"	11		Good deal of activity displayed again by both sides. Casualties. 4 Wounded (one at duty) 1 Sick	e.s.B.
"	12		In the morning we were relieved by 1/K.R.R. On relief our distribution as follows:– Bn. Hd. Qrs. C & D Coy on Keep to Annequin. A. Coy to Maison Rouge. B. Coy. 2 Platoons to Cuinchy Support Point & 2 to Railway Reserve. Cambrin Support Point 4 2 to Annequin. One man rejoined Bn.	e.s.B.

Army Form C 2118.

WAR DIARY
or
INTELLIGENCE SUMMARY
(Erase heading not required).

Instructions regarding War Diaries and Intelligence Summaries are contained in F.S. Regs., Part II and the Staff Manual respectively. Title Pages will be prepared in manuscript.

Place.	Date	Hour	Summary of Events and Information.	Remarks and references to Appendices
Annequin & vicinity.	Sep/15 13.		Clear up generally & as far as possible the Bn. rested, but mining fatigues & ammunition carrying fatigues had to be found. Casualties 2 Sick. 3 Rejoined.	C.R.B.
"	14		Mining fatigues. Casualties 1 Sick. 1 Rejoined.	C.R.B.
"	15.		Mining fatigues. Casualties 2 Sick. 3 Wounded - one of the Coys, 2/Lt. Hale died same day	C.R.B.
"	16.		Move as follows :- A & C Co. under Major Shute to Port Fixe. Bn. Hd. Qrs. B and D to Little Bethune - places at disposal of 1st Corps. Transport & Q.M. Stores remain Beuvry. M.G. Section to Cuinchy trenches.	
Bethune & Cuinchy etc.			To Bethune the men were billeted in Montmorency Barracks - Officers in the vicinity.	C.R.B.
"	17		A & C. employed on working parties B & A Company training & finding numerous coal parties to repair the vast amount of traffic made on the war. Casualties 3 Sick. 2 Rejoined.	C.R.B.

Army Form C 2118.

WAR DIARY
or
INTELLIGENCE SUMMARY
(Erase heading not required).

Instructions regarding War Diaries and Intelligence Summaries are contained in F.S. Regs., Part II and the Staff Manual respectively. Title Pages will be prepared in manuscript.

Place.	Date	Hour	Summary of Events and Information.	Remarks and references to Appendices
Bethune Cuinchy etc	Sept. 18.		A & C Cos. on working parties. B & D & Specialists Company training & Specialist training to be formed. Casualties 1 Sick. Cuinchy Posts continue	
"	19.		Working Parties found. Cuinchy Posts found. Divine Service. Casualties 3 Sick. 1 Rejoined. 2 Rejoined	G.S.B. G.S.B.
"	20.		Cuinchy Posts found. Company & Specialist training carried out. In the evening A & C Co. of Major Shute rejoined the Bn. at Bethune. Orders received that during the forthcoming operations of the Bn. will be 1. Furnishing Guards & Cuinchy Posts. 2. Taking over prisoners. 3 Supplying burial parties. This is somewhat disappointing as we had hoped for more exciting work with our Brigade. It would appear from this that we shall be again detached from 1st II Inf. Bde. Casualties 3 Sick.	
Bethune	21.		C Company proceeded to be put at the disposal of A.P.M. 2/Division. Company training carried on	G.S.B. G.S.B.

Army Form C 2118.

WAR DIARY
or
INTELLIGENCE SUMMARY
(Erase heading not required).

Instructions regarding War Diaries and Intelligence Summaries are contained in F.S. Regs., Part II and the Staff Manual respectively. Title Pages will be prepared in manuscript.

Place.	Date	Hour	Summary of Events and Information.	Remarks and references to Appendices
Bethune	Sep/15 22.		A draft of 24 men joined us. 21 of them from England of whom 9 are rheumatic, and 3 from Rouen, are old sick & wounded. Called Parts & guards furnished. Company training. Undressed Squad drill. NCOs class of instruction. Musketry on Bethune Range. Bath of B-col & German Filler. Heavy bombardment by our artillery of enemy position. Casualties 2 Sick. Rejoined.	
"	23.		Called Parts. Guards. Company training. NCOs Class of instruction. Undressed Squad drill. Musketry on Bethune Range. Casualties. One rejoined.	G.S.B.
"	24.		M.G. Section rejoins Bn in morning. 100 men of A Co. proceeded to Beuvry under 1/Corp orders. Duty- Prisoners. 100 men of B under Montmorency Beschah Beltram under 1/Corp orders - same duty. The B.M. less 100 men east of B.C. & D. Cos. moved to Gorre & Zwermoy in evening at disposal of II Division. Billets Bazziel farling road cleaning etc. Casualties. Nil men rejoined 1, & 23 joined from England of whom 8 are Rheumatic.	G.S.B. G.S.B.

WAR DIARY or INTELLIGENCE SUMMARY

Army Form C 2118.

Place	Date	Hour	Summary of Events and Information	Remarks and references to Appendices
Givenchy & Le Quesnoy	Sep 25/15		Slightly stated 5.30 A.M. with a terrific bombardment of the enemy positions. 50 men & one Officer of A Co. were sent off to East Anglian Field Co R.E. 75 men & one Officer at Givenchy to 115 Field Co. R.E. at Le Quesnoy — Both parties for road clearing duties.	
		At 7. P.M. 75 men were sent up under Capt Duncan on a burial party. We were most of the day without any reliable news of any sort. 461 German prisoners of whom 13 were Officers passed through D. Co. hands at Beuvry. The German artillery appeared very quiet from where we were; but on our front, of which there were a vast number in our vicinity, were very busy.	
		At 11 P.M. we were informed that the 100 men each of B. C. & D Cos. would rejoin the Bn. during the night, & that the Bn. would rejoin the VI Inf Bde. next morning & proceed to Cannelliere Cuinchy.	
	26.	At 1.45 A.M. the M.G. Section were reamed at rest off to Cuinchy. The men of B. C. D Co rejoined during the early hours of the morning.	
		At 9.40 A.M. the Battn. less the G Section moved off & were distributed as follows:-	G.S.R.3.

WAR DIARY
or
INTELLIGENCE SUMMARY

(Erase heading not required).

Army Form C 2118.

Place.	Date	Hour.	Summary of Events and Information.	Remarks and references to Appendices
	Sep 26 Continued		Bn. Hd. Qrs. at the old VI Inf. Bde Hd. Qrs. at Cambrin. A & C. Cos to Pont Fixe. B & D Cos to Cambrin Support Point. We are now in Brigade Reserve. Grave digging fatigues found.	
			Fighting continues. A number of 1/Kings & 2/S. Staffs dead including 4 Officers of 1/Kings and his of S. Staffs were brought down to us for burial. Heavy rain which does not add to the cheerfulness of the situation. Cambrin. 2 Sick. 1 Wounded at duty.	Q&3
Cambrin & Guinchy.	Sep 27		Fighting continues. Grave digging & burying fatigues. Large fatigue found for carrying up of smoke helmets.	
		About 4.30 P.M.	received orders that VI Bde would launch a gas attack. Bn. Hd. Qrs. went up to the trenches, also A. & C. Cos under Major Poole. Then companies being in support of 2/S. Staffs. B. & D. remained at Cambrin to be in support of 1/Kings. Our orders were to assault, if the gas was successful, otherwise not to press the attack. Gas attack a dismal failure: enemy lit fires along their parapet which appeared to dispense the gas & they eventually went to the "Wash-out". The Bn was now ordered	

WAR DIARY
or
INTELLIGENCE SUMMARY
(Erase heading not required).

Army Form C 2118.

Place.	Date	Hour	Summary of Events and Information.	Remarks and references to Appendices
Cambrin & Givinchy	Sept. 27th	continued.	to remain in readiness & to be prepared for a counter-attack. After a considerable wait it became apparent that the enemy was not going to counter attack so we returned to our previous trenches & at about 6 p.m. were again relieved by the enemy fire, both artillery and rifle, and to the time. Heavy rain fell, making it trenches very slippery indeed. Casualties. One man wounded — at duty.	G.S.B.
	Sept. 28.		Spent digging & building fire-steps. Sniping continues to the forefront. Very quiet. Heavy rain. Casualties — one wounded.	G.S.B.
	Sept. 29.		Mould out in the Givinchy trenches relieving 1/King's in Section A.2. wing from 2nd Bronx R.? Slightly uneventful but on far as we are concerned, except for a little enemy shelling & a good deal of our own, things were very quiet. Casualties 3 Rank — 10 ouded & at duty.	G.S.B.
	Sept. 30.		Things remarked at 12 noon that the G's Pile will relieve VI Bde. during the day. We were relieved by 9th Cheshires commencing at 7 p.m. but relief was not completed until 11 p.m. It was very dark & there was heavy rain, & some of the Cheshires got badly lost in the trenches. They moved lining instructions will be had to direct them & Faubourg d'annes, Bitherne & we eventually got into our billets. 1:30 A.M.	G.S.B.

6th Infantry Brigade.
2nd Division.

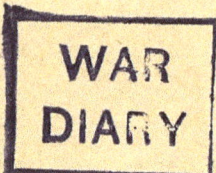

5th BATTN. THE KING'S (LIVERPOOL REGIMENT).

O C T O B E R

1 9 1 5

Army Form C 2118.

WAR DIARY
or
INTELLIGENCE SUMMARY
(Erase heading not required).

Place.	Date Oct. 1915	Hour	Summary of Events and Information.	Remarks and references to Appendices
BETHUNE.	1.		Orders received for VI Inf. Bde. to proceed to a new section of the line east of Vermelles. Colonel Martin Leake proceeded in advance to reconnoitre the position to be taken up by Bn. at 5 p.m. the Bn. marched off from Bethune under Maj Shute and arrived at Vermelles at 8 p.m. was met by Colonel Martin Leake & got into position two miles east of Vermelles by 11.15 p.m. Orders were verbally & not of a written distribution laid. Telephone wires. We relieved the 5/Rl Lancs. distribution of Bde. as follows:- 1st King's and 6/Rifles in front line — in captured German trenches. 5/Scots. 1 Hvts. in support — in front British trenches. 2/S. Staffs. 1 R. Berks in Btn. reserve in Vermelles. During the night heavy & intermittent shelling by both sides took place. Casualties — 4 Sick.	E.S.B.
Vermelles vicinity near The Dump.	2.		Heavy firing & bombing in vicinity on our left — principally in front of The Dump & Fosse 8. On our right the 5th Bde. were hotly engaged in vicinity of Gun Trench. at 6 p.m. received intimation that 1/Guards Brigade would relieve VI Bde. to-morrow. at 9 p.m. received following message from VI Bde.:- "Situation about Big Willie is not altogether satisfactory. 1/King's & Herts. on taking special precaution to secure their left flank. So must be prepared to render them any assistance if required and keep a sharp look out." The enemy are expected to counter-attack during night & men in readiness for this. Only shelling however took place. Two.	E.S.B.

Army Form C 2118.

WAR DIARY
or
INTELLIGENCE SUMMARY
(Erase heading not required).

Instructions regarding War Diaries and Intelligence Summaries are contained in F.S. Regs., Part II and the Staff Manual respectively. Title Pages will be prepared in manuscript.

Place.	Date	Hour	Summary of Events and Information.	Remarks and references to Appendices
Vermelles & vicinity of The Dump.	Oct 3rd 15		A great deal of shelling by both sides. The Bn. was warned to keep an especially sharp look-out in case enemy attacked. At 2 p.m. enemy shelled our right front-line viz. 1 KRR much hand fighting on our left in vicinity of Big Willie. 2/Grenadier Guards relieved us in evening, and on relief Bn. which moved to billets in Bethune occupying billets vi½ 1 Batt. & numerous details, Feuillade Barracks. Arrived at Bethune 11 P.M. Our casualties were 6 wounded and 1 sick. We were lucky to get off with so few casualties.	G.S.R.
Bethune.	Oct 4th		Rest & clean up. Money received. At: unless anything foreseen happened to Brigade would remain in billets for some days. Casualties 3 Sick. 1 Rejoined.	G.S.R.
"	Oct 5th		Company work. 4 P.M. Wildblood rejoined from machine Gun School. Win agnes. Casualties 3 Sick. 1 Rejoined.	G.S.R.
"	Oct 6th		Company training. General Daly came round to see the Battn & said he was very pleased to have us back — he hoped this time permanently — in the Brigade. He further mentioned that we might see our share of in the Cavalry and Yeomen attack presently. Casualties 1 Sick.	G.S.R.

Army Form C 2118.

WAR DIARY
or
INTELLIGENCE SUMMARY
(Erase heading not required).

Instructions regarding War Diaries and Intelligence Summaries are contained in F.S. Regs., Part II and the Staff Manual respectively. Title Pages will be prepared in manuscript.

Place	Date October 1915	Hour	Summary of Events and Information.	Remarks and references to Appendices
Bethune	7th		Company training. Concert given by Bn. in evening in Bethune theatre to 2nd Division. Very successful. Canadian 1 Bn. 2 Rejoined.	C.R.S.
"	8.	5.30 P.M.	Company training. Orders received to move at once to a position W. of Beuvry & N. of La Bassée – Bethune Road. Collected men from the town & moved off at 6.35 P.M. arriving at position 7.30 P.M. We settled in a field with 1 K.R.R. Kings. 2 S. Staff & Welch until 11.30 P.M. At 11.30 P.M. the Bn. was ordered to contribute to billets at Bethune, we entered to billet at Le Beuvroy to be at disposal of 7/ Division the Bn. arrived at 12.20 A.M. & experienced much difficulty in obtaining billets. However by 1.30 A.M. we were settled into old places & at let down for the remainder of the night. Up to 4.30 P.M. there was heavy firing to our front, & it seems that the Germans made an attack which after some fighting was repulsed with loss to the enemy – further this was followed up by artillery & enemy & spirit was arrival there was had quiet. Le Beuvroy has been shelled rather on our day but on our arrival this had quiet ceased.	C.R.S.
Le Beuvroy	9.		Remained at Le Beuvroy awaiting orders. Canadian 1 Bn.	L.R.S.
"	10.		In the morning moved back to an old billets at Bethune after Church Parade at Le Beuvroy. Half the Bn. billeted at the billets at Collège de Jeunes Filles. Heavy gun fire all day & night – during the front. 1 Rejoined.	C.R.S.

Army Form C 2118.

WAR DIARY
or
INTELLIGENCE SUMMARY
(Erase heading not required).

Instructions regarding War Diaries and Intelligence Summaries are contained in F.S. Regs., Part II and the Staff Manual respectively. Title Pages will be prepared in manuscript.

Place	Date Oct 1915	Hour	Summary of Events and Information.	Remarks and references to Appendices
Bethune	11		Company training carried out. Remainder of Bn. betted at Colleges de Jeunes filles.	G.R.B.
"	12		Orders received to be ready to move at 2 hour notice. Company training, & training in bombing carried out. Casualties 2 Sick. 1 Rejoined.	G.R.B.
"	13		Enemy shelled Bethune during the evening, causing a number of casualties. Very heavy artillery - probably 15" or 17". Company training & bombing carried out. Casualties — 2 Sick.	G.R.B.
"	14		Company training & bombing. Casualties — 1 Sick.	G.R.B.
"	15		Company training & bombing. Casualties — 1 Sick. 14 Rejoined.	G.R.B.
"	16		Company training & bombing practice. Draft of 42 men from 3/5 & 1st Bn R. Wheaton joined the Bn. 5 Sick. Casualties —	G.R.B.
"	17		VI Sg Bde 4st Bn 4 1 K.R.R. 2 S. Staff. 1 R. Berks. 1 Herts move to Connechem & vicinity. 1/King & ourselves remaining in Bethune. Divine Service. Casualties 2 Sick	G.R.B.

Army Form C 2118.

WAR DIARY
or
INTELLIGENCE SUMMARY
(Erase heading not required).

Instructions regarding War Diaries and Intelligence Summaries are contained in F.S. Regs., Part II and the Staff Manual respectively. Title Pages will be prepared in manuscript.

Place	Date Oct.	Hour	Summary of Events and Information.	Remarks and references to Appendices
Béthune	18.	9.15	Company training & bombing.	G.S.B.
"	19.		Company training & bombing.	G.S.B.
"	20.		Company training. Bomb Practice. Cavaliers. One sick.	
			Orders received to proceed to-morrow to Inverness. Cuinchy & take over the line from Cuinchy Street to Ridley Walk both inclusive from elements of 19th and 83 Brigades.	
			Cavaliers. 3 Sick.	G.S.B.
"	21		Bn. left Ferrillade Barracks, Béthune at 8 A.M. and relieved K.O.S.L.I. from Ridley Walk to La Brasse – Béthune Rd. and Cameronians from Stream to Cuin Street at Cuinchy between 10 A.M. & 11.30 A.M. 2.M Stores & Transport moved to Beuvry. M.G. Section to Windies leaving Reserve Stores billeted in Harley Street.	
"	22		Rather a dis-turbed day. Great deal of shelling. Casualties – No 2332 Rfn Comrie & No 1702 Rfn Fleet unfortunately killed by shell fire. One wounded. One sick.	G.S.B.

Stationery Services Press, X. 8, 5,000 7/15

Army Form C 2118.

WAR DIARY
or
INTELLIGENCE SUMMARY
(Erase heading not required).

Instructions regarding War Diaries and Intelligence Summaries are contained in F.S. Regs., Part II and the Staff Manual respectively. Title Pages will be prepared in manuscript.

Place	Date	Hour	Summary of Events and Information.	Remarks and references to Appendices
	October 1915			
Cuinchy.	22.		On usual duty. The day passed fairly quietly, but during the night but sides were obliterated [?] mortars.	
		6 P.M. to 6.30 P.M.	The enemy was very noisy shouting & laughing. They jeered lustily at our Very lights, which vicinity and somewhat later completed to their own.	e.s.B.
	23.		Usual duty. Enemy action but mortars & bombs to which we replied vigorously. One of our heavy batteries did some excellent shooting against enemy front line. Casualties – No sick.	e.s.B.
	24.		Bn. relieved by 1/ Herts R. Bellin. 4 P.M. & 5 P.M. On relief Bn. less M.G. Section marched to billets at Annequin. Billets very poor & all much crowded. Casualties – 2 sick.	e.s.B.
Annequin	25.		Numerous working parties were asked for R.E. but these were cancelled owing to the heavy rain.	
			Casualties 2 Sick. 1 Rejoined.	
"	26.		Practically whole Bn employed on R.E. working parties. Casualties 1 Sick. 1 Wounded.	e.s.B.
"	27.		During morning furnished R.E. working parties. At 2.P.M. relieved 1/K.R.R. in Support Area. Distribution as follows:—	e.s.B.

WAR DIARY
or
INTELLIGENCE SUMMARY

Army Form C 2118.

Place.	Date	Hour	Summary of Events and Information.	Remarks and references to Appendices
Cuinchy.	Oct. 27		Continued. Bn. Hd. Qrs. at 7. Harley Street. A.C. Point. Fire north side of canal. B.C. north side of canal. C.C. 3 Platoons Braddell Point & one at Cambrin. D.C. 2 Platoon Cambrin Support Point & 2 at Cuinchy Support Point. Baths for Specialists at Brigade Baths - Harley Street. Casualties - 2 Sick.	
"	28.		All available men employed during morning on R.E. working parties. B.C. & part of A. Coy. billets at Harley Street. Casualties 2 Sick. 1 Wounded but at duty.	
"	29.		Working parties during morning. C.D. & remainder of A Coy. also M.G. Sec. billeted	
"	30		Relieved 1/R. Berks in trenches. Section A.1. Cuinchy. Trenches in a result of recent heavy rain in shocking state - in many places, including front trench, fallen in. Sand bags appear to make a very bad revet-ment in wet weather & it would be worth trying hurdle work revet-ments in lieu. Casualties 1 wounded 1 regained.	
"	31.		Trench duty. Very quiet. Casualties 3 Sick.	

6th Infantry Brigade.
2nd Division.

WAR DIARY

5th BATTN. THE KING'S (LIVERPOOL REGIMENT).

NOVEMBER

1915

Army Form C. 2118

WAR DIARY No A 92 9/8 (cont.) 21

INTELLIGENCE SUMMARY

D.A.A.G. 3rd Brigade.

I forward herewith the war diary for the Bn. under my command for November 1915.
Kindly acknowledge receipt.

Lt Col [signature]
Major
Comdg. 5/8 Essex R.

11/12/15.

Place	Date Nov.	Hour		Remarks and references to Appendices
Cuinchy	1		Bn. at trenches at Cuinchy, this Coy. being employed carrying in [?] ammunition & kept at work fatigues.	
"	2		Bn. relieved by 1st R. Berks & on [?] Cuinchy.	... of heavy rain, another futile fall ... effort made to ... E.S.B.
Beuvry	3		Draft of 22 men wounded rejoined Coy.	E.S.B.
Beuvry	4		Company training	7 men sick & ... E.S.B.
Busnettes	5		12 n. relieved by [?] arrived at [?] billets at Cons, & Busnes Russell house	... smothers, returning party of ... day finding ... E.S.B.

Army Form C. 2118

Instructions regarding War Diaries and Intelligence Summaries are contained in F. S. Regs., Part II. and the Staff Manual respectively. Title Pages will be prepared in manuscript.

Place	Date Nov.	Hour	Summary of Events and Information	Remarks and references to Appendices
Cuinchy	1.		Bn. in trenches Section A.1. Cuinchy - "Ridley Walk" to "Gun Street" Trenches, tho' free of communication in very bad state as result of heavy rain. Men employed continuously repairing them. As one portion repaired another falls in. Admirable work of damage and parados of most parapets. Every effort made to keep collected fire of windy fire. Casualties: Sick 1. Rejoined 1.	C.S.B.
"	2.		Bn. relieved by 1/Herts R. and on relief went back to billets at Beuvry. Up to time of relief worked on repairs. Bde. sent up a working party of 1 I.R. Berks to assist. Casualties: Sick 3.	
Beuvry	3.		Draft of 22 men joined, of which 15 came from England 4 7 men sick 4 wounded rejoined.	C.S.B.
Beuvry	4.		Company training. Casualties: Sick 2. Rejoined 1.	C.S.B.
Busnettes	5.	12 n.	Relieved by 5th Scottish Rifles & moved to billets at Busnettes, refusing on arrival to XIX Bde. to whom we were "attached" for the day pending arrival at Gorrenchon of our own Brigade. 1/8th Russell moved to St Venant for 1 day. Guns in 4 fd. bde. mortar	C.S.B.

Army Form C. 2118

WAR DIARY
or
INTELLIGENCE SUMMARY
(Erase heading not required.)

Instructions regarding War Diaries and Intelligence Summaries are contained in F. S. Regs., Part II and the Staff Manual respectively. Title Pages will be prepared in manuscript.

Place	Date Nov.	Hour	Summary of Events and Information	Remarks and references to Appendices
Busnettes	6.		Company training. 4 C.O.s Inspection of all Companies as to arms & equipment. General results fairly satisfactory but absence of Coy badges & little drill noticeable.	e.s.B.
"	7		Church Parade.	e.s.B.
"	8		Company training started definitely 7.15 – 7.30 am Physical drill. 9.30 am – 12.30 pm under Coy Comdrs. C.O. inspected Transport as to equipment & personnel. Lieut Russell proceeded to Bde. Hd Qrs. Somewhere to take over 4 Pdr. Battery Trench Mortars. 2/Lieut Bond and 4 N.C.O.s proceeded to Somewhere for course of instruction in bombing	e.s.B.
"	9.		Company training. Casualties. Sick 2.	e.s.s.
"	10.		Company training. Very wet. Casualties. Sick 2. Rejoined 1.	e.s.B.

1875 Wt. W593/826 1,000,000 4/15 J.B.C. & A. A.D.S.S./Forms/C. 2118.

Army Form C. 2118

WAR DIARY
or
INTELLIGENCE SUMMARY
(Erase heading not required.)

Instructions regarding War Diaries and Intelligence Summaries are contained in F. S. Regs., Part II. and the Staff Manual respectively. Title Pages will be prepared in manuscript.

Place	Date Nov	Hour	Summary of Events and Information	Remarks and references to Appendices
Busnettes	11		Company training. Inspection of transport by Col and Brooks A.S.C. Verbal statement of Lieut Athelton, on transport Officer, quite satisfactory. Casualties. Sich. 1.	C.S.B.
"	12		C.O., Major Woodhouse, Lt. Keel & Q.M. left by motor at 8.30 A.M. to reconnoitre new line to be taken over by the Brigade. In line at present held by 3.6th Inf. Bde. - near Vermelles. Weather very wet & windy. All men of Bn. proceeded to Gonnehem to Rothes Vans & at same time were issued with clean clothes. Casualties. Sich 2.	C.S.B.
Bethune	13		Bn. moved from Busnettes at 2 P.M. & arrived Bethune 4.30 P.M. Billeting in Rue de Bruay area. Casualties. Sich 5. Rejoined 1.	C.S.B.
Vermelles Trenches	14	10.30 A.M.	Bn. moved to Vermelles arriving 2 P.M. & took on Support trench from 11th Middlesex R. "D" Co. being placed at disposal of 1 R. Berks R. in front line to strengthen them. Enemy shelled us intermittently from 3 P.M. to 5 P.M. Casualties. Sich 5. Rejoined 2.	C.S.B.

Army Form C. 2118

WAR DIARY
or
INTELLIGENCE SUMMARY
(Erase heading not required.)

Place	Date	Hour	Summary of Events and Information	Remarks and references to Appendices
VERMELLES	15.		Major General Walker V.C. cmdg II Division inspected the line. Inspected R.E. working parties. Enemy shelled the line intermittently during day. One artillery opened very heavy fire on enemy. Cavalier. Such 4.	C.S.S.
"	16.		R.E. Working parties furnished. Time employed laying down flare boards in communication trenches. Very quiet. Cavalier. Such 3.	C.C.S.
"	17.		Bn. relieved by 1/Herts R. in support line & in the line & in front line. Section L. 4. from "Kaiserin" retired V/R Barker R. Trench is part of the trench "Kaiserin trench" to middle of "Mud Trench" which was captured from the Germans, including the British part of Hohenzollern Redoubt. Trench is in a very bad state being deep in mud & water, except when line & trench boards had been put down. There were many of the British dead lost in the attack a month ago lying out, also in front of Rifles, Mons, & equipment. There lying about in front & every direction. Must have been during the day and brought in every night. Casualties. Wounded 1 Erich S. Rejonnds.	C.S.S.

Place	Date	Hour	Summary of Events and Information	Remarks and references to Appendices
Vermelles	Nov 17	Continued.—	There is very little wire in front of our line and there is little wire in front of the enemy, what there is varies from 60 yds to 120 yds from us, but there on the old German communication trenches running from our front line to the enemy. The ground immediately behind the German front line rather away & we are of opinion that their front line is only lightly held & that their main line is behind down the slope. A good deal of artillery fire by both sides during the day. On our left are the 2/R Staff R. & on our right the 5/R Berks of 12th Division. Front during night:— Secured — No 3075 Pte Evans.	E.S.B.
	18		All arms fully employed strengthening position & cleaning & cleaning. Rained. 2/Lt. McIntosh & No 2890 Rfn Griffiths A.C. went out during the night in patrol of bombers in some useful information regarding the enemy wire & trenches. Casualties. Wounded 1. Sick 4. Secured. No 3876 Rfn Evans. 3376 Rfn Scotland died from wounds sustained.	E.S.B.

WAR DIARY or INTELLIGENCE SUMMARY

Army Form C. 2118

Place	Date	Hour	Summary of Events and Information	Remarks and references to Appendices
Vermelles Trenches	19.		Again heavy work on repairing trenches & getting out wire entanglement during night.	e.s.r.
Bernry.	20.		Relieved by 1/1 Kings & on relief to Bn. proceeded to billets at Bernry. Sick 1. Regained 1. Sceond. Pte. 3376 Rfn. Ireland, wounded on 18 inst. unfortunately died.	e.s.r
Bernry	21.		Rest & baths for whole Bn. 1st Divisional Baths Bernry. Casualties — Sick 4 Rejoined 1.	e.s.r
"	22.		Company training. 2/Lt. McIntosh appointed Bn. Transport Officer vice 2nd Lt. Oldelation rejoining his Co. on 9.9.15 in Command. Casualties — Sick 4. Rejoined 1.	e.s.r.B.
Vermelles Trenches	23.		Relieved 1/Herts R. in Sec. Z.O. ("Mud Trench" to "R 1".) 2/S. Staff R. on our right. 1 R. Berks R. on our left. Near three Cos. in front line with C Co. in support. 9 wd. during night. Casualties Sick 5. Rejoined 3.	e.s.rB.
"	24.		Trench duties. A.Co. 18 R. Fusiliers came to us for training in trench warfare. They took over the head of our trench occupied by D. Co who went back to the Factory Dug Out. A German approached down to our front line & was fired at & fell. A scout was made for him but without result. Eventually he was wounded & escaped by a German Sap which came to within 75 yds of our trench. Sent during night.	e.s.rB.

WAR DIARY
or
INTELLIGENCE SUMMARY
(Erase heading not required.)

Army Form C. 2118

Place	Date	Hour	Summary of Events and Information	Remarks and references to Appendices
Vermelles Sunday	Nov. 25th		Trench duty. Snowed during night - also frost. Casualties - Sick 4.	G.S.B.
Bewry	26.		Relieved by 1/Herts R & on relief proceeded to billets at Bewry. Snowed during night & again heavily during our march back. Casualties - Wounded 1. Sick 1. Rejoined 3.	G.S.B.
Bewry	27.		Clean up of kit inspection. Invented R.E. working parties. In afternoon C.O. played B vs Bn. football tournament & in the evening we had a concert. Casualties Sick 2. Rejoined 2.	G.S.B.
"	28.		Church Parade. O/C Royce rejoined Bn. from IV Inf. Bde. where he had been acting as Bde. Signal Officer (latter for all men of Bewry Divisional baths). In the evening we had a concert. Casualties - Sick 3.	G.S.B.
"	29.		Bn. was ordered to relieve 1 K.R.R. in Cambrin trenches but at the last moment this was cancelled owing to heavy bombardment & relief ordered to take place to-morrow. Company training. Football match in evening followed by a concert. Casualties - Wounded 1. Sick 4. Rejoined 2.	G.S.B.

Army Form C. 2118

WAR DIARY
or
INTELLIGENCE SUMMARY

(Erase heading not required.)

Instructions regarding War Diaries and Intelligence Summaries are contained in F.S. Regs., Part II. and the Staff Manual respectively. Title Pages will be prepared in manuscript.

Place	Date. Nov	Hour	Summary of Events and Information	Remarks and references to Appendices
Cambrin Trenches	30.		Relieved 1/K.R.R. in Cambrin Trenches Section Z.1. ("Point R.1. to "Point D.") D. Co. 22. R F. position was started to in cleaning & 24 hours - on positions being started to east of our Companies. Removed to trenches in a very bad state. All men continuously employed cleaning & repairing them. Casualties. Rank 1.	C.S.R.

1875 Wt. W 593/826 1,000,000 4/15 J.B.C. & A. A.D.S.S./Forms/C. 2118.

6th Infantry Brigade.

2nd Division.

(Battn. transferred to
99th Bde. 2nd Div.
15.12.15)

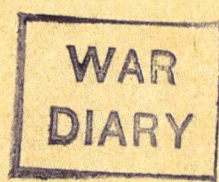

5th BATTN. THE KING'S (LIVERPOOL REGIMENT).

D E C E M B E R

1 9 1 5

Attached:

Patrol Report
21.12.15.

WAR DIARY or INTELLIGENCE SUMMARY

Army Form C. 2118

(Erase heading not required.)

Place	Date	Hour	Summary of Events and Information	Remarks and references to Appendices
CAMBRIN	Dec 1st		The Battalion was in the trenches in Z1. Beoy 22 Royal Fusiliers were relieved by "D" Coy 22 Royal Fusiliers for instruction under us and were placed in front trench relieving our Coy but under the supervision of Maj Worsdale OC "C" Coy. The round successively the trenches fell in or all sides. Everyman worked on keeping the trenches open. Col. McMaster went on leave & Maj Pratt took over the command of the Battalion.	
"	Dec 2nd		"D" Coy 22 R F relieved their B Coy now taken as a Stch Coy under Maj Worsdale.	
"	Dec 3.		"D" Coy 22 R F rejoined their unit. "C" Coy took over that part of the line. The Batt: lost 2 men killed by rifle fire.	
"	Dec 4		Rain continues the whole time. Owing mainly to the rate at which the trenches were falling in. The Batt: at the critical time were unable to get any trench boards, although the necessity for them had been strongly pointed out. Revetting everywhere is considered necessary as the earth is loose crumbling mud. Had rain. The Batt. was relieved by the 1/Kings & proceed to billets in Beuvry.	

WAR DIARY or INTELLIGENCE SUMMARY

Army Form C. 2118

Place	Date	Hour	Summary of Events and Information	Remarks and references to Appendices
BEUVRY	Dec 5		The Batt: having come out of the trenches up to the ears in mud the day before, consequently all day was given up to cleaning up with the exception of an hour for Divine Service. There was a football match in the afternoon received with great joy.	
—	Dec 6		The men all went to the Divisional Baths which were very much appreciated. Great difficulty is experienced in getting the men off the greatcoats & heavy linen trousers not to take them into the trenches & to rely on their leather jerkins to keep them warm.	
CAMBRIN	Dec 7	4 AM.	The Batt: relieved the 1/KRRC in CAMBRIN trenches 22. (G₁₁ G1 to G Boyau 15). The trenches were just passable. Floor boards which had been laid were in many places covered up by enormous landslides. The Germans fired on trench mortar which landed in the trench blowing the sentry over the parapet. He was killed.	
—	Dec 8		A good deal of sniping by the enemy. Our own sniped. The succeeding work of keeping the trenches clear still going on.	

WAR DIARY
or
INTELLIGENCE SUMMARY

Army Form C. 2118

Place	Date	Hour	Summary of Events and Information	Remarks and references to Appendices
CAMBLIN.	Dec 9.		Capt. Buckley + 9 NCO's & middlesex kept in or attached to us for training. They actually serve till after dark + so had to wait till the following day. Very quiet in front, the hostile snipers having died down.	
	Dec 10.		The Batt. was relieved by the 1 KRRC + proceeded to shelters in BEUVRY. The trenches were again in a very bad condition. In some cases been having to leave their firm bolts behind stuck in the mud.	
BEUVRY.	Dec 11.		All men went to the Divisional baths + had clean changes of underclothing. Kit inspection.	
	Dec 12.		Divine service. In the afternoon J. Coy played the Transport section at football. The match was played on a field what had been a field row a swamp. The match was much enjoyed by everyone.	
CAMBLIN.	Dec 13.		Relieved the 1 KRRC in the trenches in Z. (A1 - Boyan (s). The pry in the trenches was very bad in parts. The men worked all night bringing up floor boards on the Railway + working in the trenches. The Railway ran from the Sylt. of Cambrin Church by the Soup Kitchen to our keep. Frosty night. + moonlight. Hostile snipers free active harassing our line.	

1875 Wt. W593/826 1,000,000 4/15 J.B.C. & A. A.D.S.S./Forms/C. 2118.

Army Form C. 2118

WAR DIARY
or
INTELLIGENCE SUMMARY
(Erase heading not required.)

Instructions regarding War Diaries and Intelligence Summaries are contained in F.S. Regs., Part II. and the Staff Manual respectively. Title Pages will be prepared in manuscript.

Place	Date	Hour	Summary of Events and Information	Remarks and references to Appendices
CAMISRIN	Dec 14th		All Coys busily employed getting rid in their trenches, carrying of away mud timber stretchers. The enemy shelled tonabat Sings KEEP trying in vain to hit the Railway. The night was very quiet + a large quantity of steel boards, steel wire in sheaf decamp were brought up on the Railway.	
	Dec 15.		The day was a fine one with a fresh SW wind. We were warned to find two raiding parties to raid the enemy's trenches after artillery had been used. The latter was to be enrolled in great volume. 11 A.M. Wbg. Coys cut the German wire. The German Whg bays retaliated on our support trenches. Operations were arranged down to the smallest detail by the Batt.	
		9.40 P.M.	Toby Wann. "Operations postponed." Everything readjusted. Banks returned.	
			Machine Guns changed.	
		6.15 P.M.	Orders received to hand over "B" spherical HE too left to travel a scoopful of order being repeated to pellet brain. Bond mistated gaps officers seen, a the matter was found. The Ante diaries self Very much by officers there.	
	Midnight.		Operation finish declared off. Rain falling.	

Army Form C. 2118

WAR DIARY
or
INTELLIGENCE SUMMARY
(Erase heading not required.)

Place	Date	Hour	Summary of Events and Information	Remarks and references to Appendices
CAMBRIN.	15/16	12 mid night.	The 99th Bde. took over from the 6th Bde. & from that time the 5th Kings Liverpool belongs to the 99th Bde.	
—	Dec 16.		A very quiet day compared to yesterday. The enemy shelling & very little of our own. All Coys busy working on the floors of their trenches, & laying trench boards which were in as pheu. a demand as usual. The RE were especially conspicuous by their absence. No doubt they were working in the rear sector, but all Batt think their sector to be the worst.	
—	Day 7.		Relieved by Royal Half Batt, HARR. Took over from 2 half Batts in Annequin. To get over to big problem of how to get rid of thousand & the trenches or oflaried trench stretchers from the R.E. & scarped the turf in marril d'away to suitable places. All of the trench to poles & disused trenches. Resting and cleaning up. The weather was wet but very mild.	
ANNEQUIN S.	Dec. 8.			
—	Dec. 9.		Church Parade in the field closed at 10.30. The R.C. marched to Beuvry. The hysll was very disturbed by bursts of fire from the 4.7 ins artillery every two hours.	

Army Form C. 2118

WAR DIARY
or
INTELLIGENCE SUMMARY
(Erase heading not required.)

Place	Date	Hour	Summary of Events and Information	Remarks and references to Appendices
CAM/15/R.I.N.	Dec 20		Relieved the 22 RF in the trenches in Z0, marched out of Annequin. South at 6AM + relieved at 8AM. This early relief was necessary owing to a protracted bombardment by the 47th Div. which district. takes place. The Batt! marched into the trenches with about 1/2 the strength to the 22 RF. The RF were very slow in moving out. In the evening we had to prepare for the gas attack. The raiding party comprised 24 NCO's + men + 2 Officers of the 22 RF whereas to go out from the trap on the left of the RF. Raid. We reported every lashed wire was still intact. Conditions are un- favourable - nothing took place. We found the trenches had been allowed to fall into a very bad condition. On the left is 21 work + Batt R.R.R. On the Right is 1/4 work the 23 London Cy London.	
	Dec 21st		The weather became much better. We were provided Working parties from the Batt. which bent hitself up + which was behind 5 from gone to Z1. Communication trench N°2 from the Right Front Cy to the Reserve trench was a ruin when we arrived + has been ordered to be block it up. We took it in hand + cleared the able trench laying floor boards. The light was clear + searchlight, the wind favourable. The gas weather	

Army Form C. 2118

WAR DIARY
or
INTELLIGENCE SUMMARY
(Erase heading not required.)

Place	Date	Hour	Summary of Events and Information	Remarks and references to Appendices
CAMBRIN.			at 9P.M. Our own raiding party under Lt. Reid. Apparently the Germans laughed at the gas for the klaxons and machine gun fire went on all the time. The enemy sent up red lights + lit fires all along their parapet. Gas is on. They sent up green ones which seemed to indicate that an attack was expected. About 10 seconds after the gas started to go off (Zero), the enemy opened a very heavy bombardment from all types of guns. This only lasted for about 10 minutes. We sent out a patrol (Sheen) who saw a German patrol of 10 men in the distance. Our own party had and reported it. Other men went out and attempted to work the German sap. The party found the sap well held + strong (hints his?) Two of which only went off. It was found that there was to have been a sap and the spring, which had become bad with the wet weather that prevented them going up.	
		9P.M.	A quiet day. A large working party of the 22 R.F. came up to help a clean up + dig afterwards in trenches. The Vii Division took over Givenchy left of their pass which appeared to go on very	

Place	Date	Hour	Summary of Events and Information	Remarks and references to Appendices
CAMBRIN			10th. The enemy again let fires on our left. We were subjected to an intense bombardment for 10 minutes. From different calibre guns. The 15 Battery replied.	
	Dec 23.		The Batt was relieved by the 22 RF between 2-3 o'clock PM. The morning had been quiet. Rain but the rain came on at 5 PM & the Batt marched back to billets in Annequin South in the pelting rain. The T.O. Chaplain visited came up to the trenches earlier and the day had their horses wounded under them by shrapnel.	
ANNEQUIN S.	Dec 24.		Cleaning up & making preparations for xmas. Then small working parties of 15 men each formed for cleansing then Ration stores for Divs kept in 2i. One officer & 30 Grenadiers went for instruction in bombing in the trenches between Annequin & Beuvry.	
	Dec 25.		Xmas day. The weather was an exception to the rule. The whole Batt went out at 7AM to clean MAISON ROUGE & BURBURE ALLY. They returned at noon. In order to celebrate xmas & to distrest all thoughts of war, an Xmas dinner was arranged for the men. They then sat down in two tables the 1st party at 6 o'clock the second at 8 o'clock. Before the dinner commenced	

WAR DIARY or INTELLIGENCE SUMMARY

Army Form C. 2118

Place	Date	Hour	Summary of Events and Information	Remarks and references to Appendices
ANNEQUIN S.	Dec 26		Brig. General Kellett & Col. Vaughn (chief of Divisional Staff) came round & inspected the trenches. It was evident that they were accepted although had been achieved in this 2600 yds of the line front. General Kellett spoke a few words of praise & welcome as he passed through each town.	
CAMBRIN.	Dec 26		The Batt. relieved the 2/RF in Z.20. The line was all in very good shirts. The previous day had certainly done much to improve the moral of the troops. On our right were the 1 Cavalry of London, on our left 1/2 Batt KRR. The day was quiet & succeeded to be wet. At night the Left Front Coy was rather disturbed by hostile rifle grenades. The 17 Better was called upon whose silenced them.	
	Dec 27		More rain at intervals. Working parties were out all day clearing & repairing land slides. At night there was a great deal of machine gun fire on both sides, but this cole being able to silence another.	
	Dec 28	9.50AM	The enemy shelled near Hy Kerf. The shells were thought to come from their armoured train. They definitely again at noon.	

Army Form C. 2118

WAR DIARY
or
INTELLIGENCE SUMMARY
(Erase heading not required.)

Place	Date	Hour	Summary of Events and Information	Remarks and references to Appendices
Cam R.W.	29.		The Batt was relieved by the 1st Batt Cameronians. 19 Bde 33 Div. The Batt went into billets at ANNEQUIN SOUTH.	
	30.		The Batt marched back to its billets, in the D'AIRE BETHUNE. The men seemed very little refreshed very weary. In the afternoon the Baths at the École de Jeunes Filles were at the disposal of the Batt. In the evening the men went to the 2 Div Pantomime "The Babes in the Wood".	
	31st.		The day was devoted to cleaning up & refreshing the men, most of whom were badly in need of new clothes last after our breaks of 3 days in & 3 days out of the trenches.	

Chas J Shute
Lieut Col
O.C. 5th Liverpool Reg.

PATROL REPORT 21.12.15.

PATROL REPORT.
****

5th Kings (L'pool) Regt.
   Report on Patrol 21/12/15.

At about 10.15 p.m., three men left our trench where it crosses the Railway and proceeded along the Railway toward the German trench. They reached a point 40 or 50 yards out, near the German Saphead, and were fired on from the German front line trench. At the same time they saw about 10 Germans get out of the front trench, some 50 yards from them and proceed towards the left, i.e. towards Z.1. The K.R.R.C were warned of this immediately. The patrol also reported that they could hear men moving about in the German trench and sap. At about 10.50 p.m. they went out again and thr[ew] 3 bombs at the German Saphead, only two of which exploded, one in the Saphead. They were again fired on from the fro[nt] trench. They reported that the German trench seemed full of men and they heard sounds of talking, whistling and knocking, besides seeing the heads of several men above the trench. They also heard men in the Sap. They came in at 11.20 p.m.

The light was too bright for anything further to be done.

(Sd) ALEX. REID. Lt.
     5th Kings (L'Pool) Regt.

www.ingramcontent.com/pod-product-compliance
Lightning Source LLC
Chambersburg PA
CBHW081425160426
43193CB00013B/2195